NATURE OF THE SECOND SEX

In a rapidly changing world the basic needs of men and women remain the same. These needs are often submerged and only partially understood. Simone de Beauvoir exposes the myths that still haunt our lives, discusses the dreams and fears that are legacies from earlier ages, dissects the opposing views of the psychologists that add to our confusion and in clear, incisive terms examines the biological facts.

'There is no doubt that this is an important and serious study.'

The Times Literary Supplement

*Also by Simone de Beauvoir and available in the
    Four Square series*

THE SECOND SEX
The companion to this volume

**BRIGITTE BARDOT AND THE LOLITA SYN-
    DROME**
Profusely illustrated

DJAMILA BOUPACHA
With Gisèle Halimi

Nature of the
SECOND SEX

SIMONE
De BEAUVOIR

Translated from the French
and edited by H. M. Parshley

A FOUR SQUARE BOOK

Originally published in France by Librairie Gallimard in 1949
under the title *Le Deuxiè me Sexe* (2 vols.)
First published in Great Britain by Jonathan Cape Ltd. in 1953
Second Impression 1956

The first volume published as a Four Square Book
in 1961 under the title *A History of Sex*
Reprinted October 1961
Reprinted under the title *Nature of the Second Sex*
in September 1963

*Four Square Books are published by The New English Library Limited from Barnard's Inn,
Holborn, London EC1. They are made and printed in Great Britain by Love and
Malcomson Ltd. Redhill, Surrey*

INTRODUCTION

FOR a long time I have hesitated to write a book on woman. The subject is irritating, especially to women ; and it is not new. Enough ink has been spilled in quarrelling over feminism, and perhaps we should say no more about it. It is still talked about, however, for the voluminous nonsense uttered during the last century seems to have done little to illuminate the problem. After all, is there a problem? And if so, what is it? Are there women, really? Most assuredly the theory of the eternal feminine still has its adherents who will whisper in your ear: 'Even in Russia women still are *women*' ; and other erudite persons—sometimes the very same—say with a sigh: 'Woman is losing her way, woman is lost.' One wonders if women still exist, if they will always exist, whether or not it is desirable that they should, what place they occupy in this world, what their place should be. 'What has become of women?' was asked recently in an ephemeral magazine.

But first we must ask: what is a woman? '*Tota mulier in utero*', says one, 'woman is a womb'. But in speaking of certain women, connoisseurs declare that they are not women, although they are equipped with a uterus like the rest. All agree in recognizing the fact that females exist in the human species ; today as always they make up about one half of humanity. And yet we are told that femininity is in danger ; we are exhorted to be women, remain women, become women. It would appear, then, that every female human being is not necessarily a woman ; to be so considered she must share in that mysterious and threatened reality known as femininity. Is this attribute something secreted by the ovaries? Or is it a Platonic essence, a product of the philosophic imagination? Is a rustling petticoat enough to bring it down to earth? Although some women try zealously to incarnate this essence, it is hardly patentable. It is frequently described in vague and dazzling terms that seem to have been borrowed from the vocabulary of the seers, and indeed in the times of St. Thomas it was considered an essence as certainly defined as the somniferous virtue of the poppy.

But conceptualism has lost ground. The biological and social sciences no longer admit the existence of unchangeably fixed entities that determine given characteristics, such as those ascribed to woman, the Jew, or the Negro. Science regards any characteristic as a reaction dependent in part upon a *situation*. If today femininity no longer exists, then it never existed. But does the word *woman*, then, have no specific content? This is stoutly affirmed by those who hold to the philosophy of the enlightenment, of rationalism, of nominalism; women, to them, are merely the human beings arbitrarily designated by the word *woman*. Many American women particularly are prepared to think that there is no longer any place for woman as such; if a backward individual still takes herself for a woman, her friends advise her to be psychoanalysed and thus get rid of this obsession. In regard to a work, *Modern Woman: The Lost Sex*, which in other respects has its irritating features, Dorothy Parker has written: 'I cannot be just to books which treat of woman as woman ... My idea is that all of us, men as well as women, should be regarded as human beings.' But nominalism is a rather inadequate doctrine, and the anti-feminists have had no trouble in showing that women simply *are not* men. Surely woman is, like man, a human being; but such a declaration is abstract. The fact is that every concrete human being is always a singular, separate individual. To decline to accept such notions as the eternal feminine, the black soul, the Jewish character, is not to deny that Jews, Negroes, women exist today—this denial does not represent a liberation for those concerned, but rather a flight from reality. Some years ago a well-known woman writer refused to permit her portrait to appear in a series of photographs especially devoted to women writers; she wished to be counted among the men. But in order to gain this privilege she made use of her husband's influence! Women who assert that they are men lay claim none the less to masculine consideration and respect. I recall also a young Trotskyite standing on a platform at a boisterous meeting and getting ready to use her fists, in spite of her evident fragility. She was denying her feminine weakness; but it was for love of a militant male whose equal she wished to be. The attitude of defiance of many American women proves that they are haunted by a sense of their femininity. In truth, to go for a walk with one's eyes open is enough to demonstrate that humanity is divided into two classes of individuals whose clothes, faces, bodies, smiles, gaits, interests, and occupations are manifestly different. Perhaps these differences are superficial, perhaps they are destined to disappear. What is certain is that they do most obviously exist.

If her functioning as a female is not enough to define woman, if we decline also to explain her through 'the eternal feminine', and if nevertheless we admit, provisionally, that women do exist, then we must face the question: what is a woman?

To state the question is, to me, to suggest, at once, a preliminary answer. The fact that I ask it is in itself significant. A man would never set out to write a book on the peculiar situation of the human male. But if I wish to define myself, I must first of all say: 'I am a woman'; on this truth must be based all further discussion. A man never begins by presenting himself as an individual of a certain sex; it goes without saying that he is a man. The terms *masculine* and *feminine* are used symmetrically only as a matter of form, as on legal papers. In actuality the relation of the two sexes is not quite like that of two electrical poles, for man represents both the positive and the neutral, as is indicated by the common use of *man* to designate human beings in general; whereas woman represents only the negative, defined by limiting criteria, without reciprocity. In the midst of an abstract discussion it is vexing to hear a man say: 'You think thus and so because you are a woman'; but I know that my only defence is to reply: 'I think thus and so because it is true,' thereby removing my subjective self from the argument. It would be out of the question to reply: 'And you think the contrary because you are a man', for it is understood that the fact of being a man is no peculiarity. A man is in the right in being a man; it is the woman who is in the wrong. It amounts to this: just as for the ancients there was an absolute vertical with reference to which the oblique was defined, so there is an absolute human type, the masculine. Woman has ovaries, a uterus; these peculiarities imprison her in her subjectivity, circumscribe her within the limits of her own nature. It is often said that she thinks with her glands. Man superbly ignores the fact that his anatomy also includes glands, such as the testicles, and that they secrete hormones. He thinks of his body as a direct and normal connection with the world, which he believes he apprehends objectively, whereas he regards the body of woman as a hindrance, a prison, weighed down by everything peculiar to it. 'The female is a female by virtue of a certain *lack* of qualities,' said Aristotle; 'we should regard

7

the female nature as afflicted with a natural defectiveness.'
And St. Thomas for his part pronounced woman to be an
'imperfect man', an 'incidental' being. This is symbolized in
Genesis where Eve is depicted as made from what Bossuet
called 'a supernumerary bone' of Adam.

Thus humanity is male and man defines woman not in herself but as relative to him; she is not regarded as an autonomous being. Michelet writes: 'Women, the relative being
...' And Benda is most positive in his *Rapport d'Uriel*: 'the
body of man makes sense in itself quite apart from that of
woman, whereas the latter seems wanting in significance by
itself... Man can think of himself without woman. She cannot think of herself without man.' And she is simply what man
decrees; thus she is called 'the sex', by which is meant that she
appears essentially to the male as a sexual being. For him
she is sex—absolute sex, no less. She is defined and differentiated with reference to man and not he with reference to her;
she is the incidental, the inessential as opposed to the essential.
He is the Subject, he is the Absolute—she is the Other.[1]

The category of the *Other* is as primordial as consciousness
itself. In the most primitive societies, in the most ancient
mythologies, one finds the expression of a duality—that of the
Self and the Other. This duality was not originally attached
to the division of the sexes; it was not dependent upon any
empirical fact. It is revealed in such words as that of Granet
on Chinese thought and those of Dumézil on the East Indies
and Rome. The feminine element was at first no more

[1] E. Lévinas expresses this idea most explicitly in his essay
Temps et l'Autre. 'Is there not a case in which otherness,
alterity [*altérité*], unquestionably marks the nature of a being, as
its essence, an instance of otherness not consisting purely and
simply in the opposition of two species of the same genus? I
think that the feminine represents the contrary in its absolute
sense, this contrariness being in no wise affected by any relation
between it and its correlative and thus remaining absolutely
other. Sex is not a certain specific difference... no more is the
sexual difference a mere contradiction... Nor does this difference lie in the duality of two complementary terms, for two
complementary terms imply a pre-existing whole . . . Otherness
reaches its full flowering in the feminine, a term of the same
rank as consciousness but of opposite meaning.'
I suppose that Lévinas does not forget that woman, too, is
aware of her own consciousness, or ego. But it is striking that
he deliberately takes a man's point of view, disregarding the
reciprocity of subject and object. When he writes that woman
is mystery, he implies that she is mystery for man. Thus his
description, which is intended to be objective, is in fact an
assertion of masculine privilege.

involved in such pairs as Varuna-Mitra, Uranus-Zeus, Sun-Moon, and Day-Night than it was in the contrasts between Good and Evil, lucky and unlucky auspices, right and left, God and Lucifer. Otherness is a fundamental category of human thought.

Thus it is that no group ever sets itself up as the One without at once setting up the Other over against itself. If three travellers chance to occupy the same compartment, that is enough to make vaguely hostile 'others' out of all the rest of the passengers on the train. In small-town eyes all persons not belonging to the village are 'strangers' and suspect ; to the native of a country all who inhabit other countries are 'foreigners' ; Jews are 'different' for the anti-Semite, Negroes are 'inferior' for American racists, aborigines are 'natives' for colonists, proletarians are the 'lower class' for the privileged.

Lévi-Strauss, at the end of a profound work on the various forms of primitive societies, reaches the following conclusion: 'Passage from the state of Nature to the state of Culture is marked by man's ability to view biological relations as a series of contrasts ; duality, alternation, opposition, and symmetry, whether under definite or vague forms, constitute not so much phenomena to be explained as fundamental and immediately given data of social reality.'[1] These phenomena would be incomprehensible if in fact human society were simply a *Mitsein* or fellowship based on solidarity and friendliness. Things become clear, on the contrary, if, following Hegel, we find in consciousness itself a fundamental hostility towards every other consciousness ; the subject can be posed only in being opposed—he sets himself up as the essential, as opposed to the other, the inessential, the object.

But the other consciousness, the other ego, sets up a reciprocal claim. The native travelling abroad is shocked to find himself in turn regarded as a 'stranger' by the natives of neighbouring countries. As a matter of fact, wars, festivals, trading, treaties, and contests among tribes, nations, and classes tend to deprive the concept *Other* of its absolute sense and to make manifest its relativity ; willy-nilly, individuals and groups are forced to realize the reciprocity of their relations. How is it, then, that this reciprocity has not been recognized between the sexes, that one of the contrasting terms is set up as the sole essential, denying any relativity in regard to its correlative and defining the latter as pure otherness? Why is

[1] See C. LEVI-STRAUSS, *Les Structures élémentaires de parenté.*

it that women do not dispute male sovereignty? No subject will readily volunteer to become the object, the inessential; it is not the Other who, in defining himself as the Other, establishes the One. The Other is posed as such by the One in defining himself as the One. But if the Other is not to regain the status of being the One, he must be submissive enough to accept this alien point of view. Whence comes this submission in the case of woman?

There are, to be sure, other cases in which a certain category has been able to dominate another completely for a time. Very often this privilege depends upon inequality of numbers—the majority imposes its rule upon the minority or persecutes it. But women are not a minority, like the American Negroes or the Jews; there are as many women as men on earth. Again, the two groups concerned have often been originally independent; they may have been formerly unaware of each other's existence, or perhaps they recognized each other's autonomy. But a historical event has resulted in the subjugation of the weaker by the stronger. The scattering of the Jews, the introduction of slavery into America, the conquests of imperialism are examples in point. In these cases the oppressed retained at least the memory of former days; they possessed in common a past, a tradition, sometimes a religion or a culture.

The parallel drawn by Bebel between women and the proletariat is valid in that neither ever formed a minority or a separate collective unit of mankind. And instead of a single historical event it is in both cases a historical development that explains their status as a class and accounts for the membership of *particular individuals* in that class. But proletarians have not always existed, whereas there have always been women. They are women in virtue of their anatomy and physiology. Throughout history they have always been subordinated to men,[1] and hence their dependency is not the result of a historical event or a social change—it was not something that *occurred*. The reason why otherness in this case seems to be an absolute is in part that it lacks the contingent or incidental nature of historical facts. A condition brought about at a certain time can be abolished at some other time, as the Negroes of Haiti and others have proved; but it might seem that a natural condition is beyond the possibility of change. In truth, however, the nature of things is no more

[1] With rare exceptions, perhaps, like certain matriarchal rulers, queens, and the like.—TR.

10

immutably given, once for all, than is historical reality. If woman seems to be the inessential which never becomes the essential, it is because she herself fails to bring about this change. Proletarians say 'We'; Negroes also. Regarding themselves as subjects, they transform the bourgeois, the whites, into 'others'. But women do not say 'We', except at some congress of feminists or similar formal demonstration; men say 'women', and women use the same word in referring to themselves. They do not authentically assume a subjective attitude. The proletarians have accomplished the revolution in Russia, the Negroes in Haiti, the Indo-Chinese are battling for it in Indo-China; but the women's effort has never been anything more than a symbolic agitation. They have gained only what men have been willing to grant; they have taken nothing, they have only received.[1]

The reason for this is that women lack concrete means for organizing themselves into a unit which can stand face to face with the correlative unit. They have no past, no history, no religion of their own; and they have no such solidarity, no work and interest as that of the proletariat. They are not even promiscuously herded together in the way that creates community feeling among the American Negroes, the ghetto Jews, the workers of Saint-Denis, or the factory hands of Renault. They live dispersed among the males, attached through residence, housework, economic condition, and social standing to certain men—fathers or husbands—more firmly than they are to other women. If they belong to the bourgeoisie, they feel solidarity with men of that class, not with proletarian women; if they are white, their allegiance is to white men, not to Negro women. The proletariat can propose to massacre the ruling class, and a sufficiently fanatical Jew or Negro might dream of getting sole possession of the atomic bomb and making humanity wholly Jewish or black; but woman cannot even dream of exterminating the males. The bond that unites her to her oppressors is not comparable to any other. The division of the sexes is a biological fact, not an event in human history. Male and female stand opposed within a primordial *Mitsein*, and woman has not broken it. The couple is a fundamental unity with its two halves riveted together, and the cleavage of society along the line of sex is impossible. Here is to be found the basic trait of woman: she is the Other in a totality of which the two components are necessary to one another.

[1] See Part II, chap. v.

One could suppose that this reciprocity might have facilitated the liberation of woman. When Hercules sat at the feet of Omphale and helped with her spinning, his desire for her held him captive ; but why did she fail to gain a lasting power? To revenge herself on Jason, Medea killed their children ; and this grim legend would seem to suggest that she might have obtained a formidable influence over him through his love for his offspring. In *Lysistrata* Aristophanes gaily depicts a band of women who joined forces to gain social ends through the sexual needs of their men ; but this is only a play. In the legend of the Sabine women, the latter soon abandoned their plan of remaining sterile to punish their ravishers. In truth woman has not been socially emancipated through man's need—sexual desire and the desire for offspring—which makes the male dependent for satisfaction upon the female.

Master and slave, also, are united by a reciprocal need, in this case economic, which does not liberate the slave. In the relation of master to slave the master does not make a point of the need that he has for the other ; he has in his grips the power of satisfying this need through his own action ; whereas the slave, in his dependent condition, his hope and fear, is quite conscious of the need he has for his master. Even if the need is at bottom equally urgent for both, it always works in favour of the oppressor and against the oppressed. That is why the liberation of the working class, for example, has been slow.

Now, woman has always been man's dependent, if not his slave ; the two sexes have never shared the world in equality. And even today woman is heavily handicapped, though her situation is beginning to change. Almost nowhere is her legal status the same as man's, and frequently it is much to her disadavantage. Even when her rights are legally recognized in the abstract, long-standing custom prevents their full expression in the mores. In the economic sphere men and women can almost be said to make up two castes ; other things being equal, the former hold the better jobs, get higher wages, and have more opportunity for success than their new competitors. In industry and politics men have a great many more positions and they monopolize the most important posts. In addition to all this, they enjoy a traditional prestige that the education of children tends in every way to support, for the present enshrines the past—and in the past all history has been made by men. At the present time, when women are beginning to take part in the affairs of the world, it is still a world that belongs to men—they have no doubt of it at all and women have scarcely any. To decline to be the Other, to refuse to be a party to the deal—this would be for women to renounce all the advantages conferred upon them by their alliance with the superior caste. Man-the-sovereign will provide woman-the-liege with material protection and will undertake the moral justification of her existence; thus she can evade at once both economic risk and the metaphysical risk of a liberty in which ends and aims must be contrived without assistance. Indeed, along with the ethical urge of each individual to affirm his subjective existence, there is also the temptation to forgo liberty and become a thing. This is an inauspicious road, for he who takes it—passive, lost, ruined—becomes henceforth the creature of another's will, frustrated in his transcendence and deprived of every value. But it is an easy road; on it one avoids the strain involved in undertaking an authentic existence. When man makes of woman the *Other*, he may, then, expect her to manifest deep-seated tendencies towards complicity. Thus, woman may fail to lay claim to the status of subject because she lacks definite resources, because she feels the necessary bond that ties her to man regardless of reciprocity, and because she is often very well pleased with her role as the *Other*.

But it will be asked at once: how did all this begin? It is easy to see that the duality of the sexes, like any duality, gives rise to conflict. And doubtless the winner will assume the status of absolute. But why should man have won from the start? It seems possible that women could have won the victory; or that the outcome of the conflict might never have been decided. How is it that this world has always belonged to the men and that things have begun to change only recently? Is this change a good thing? Will it bring about an equal sharing of the world between men and women?

These questions are not new, and they have often been answered. But the very fact that woman *is the Other* tends to cast suspicion upon all the justification that men have ever been able to provide for it. These have all too evidently been dictated by men's interest. A little-known feminist of the seventeenth century, Poulain de la Barre, put it this way: 'All that has been written about women by men should be suspect, for the men are at once judge and party to the

13

lawsuit.' Everywhere, at all times, the males have displayed their satisfaction in feeling that they are the lords of creation. 'Blessed be God . . . that He did not make me a woman,' say the Jews in their morning prayers, while their wives pray on a note of resignation: 'Blessed be the Lord, who created me according to His will.' The first among the blessings for which Plato thanked the gods was that he had been created free, not enslaved; the second, a man, not a woman. But the males could not enjoy this privilege fully unless they believed it to be founded on the absolute and the eternal; they sought to make the fact of their supremacy into a right. 'Being men, those who have made and compiled the laws have favoured their own sex, and jurists have elevated these laws into principles', to quote Poulain de la Barre once more.

Legislators, priests, philosophers, writers, and scientists have striven to show that the subordinate position of woman is willed in heaven and advantageous on earth. The religions invented by men reflect this wish for domination. In the legends of Eve and Pandora men have taken up arms against women. They have made use of philosophy and theology, as the quotations from Aristotle and St. Thomas have shown. Since ancient times satirists and moralists have delighted in showing up the weaknesses of women. We are familiar with the savage indictment hurled against women throughout French literature. Montherlant, for example, follows the tradition of Jean de Meung, though with less gusto. This hostility may at times be well founded, often it is gratuitous; but in truth it more or less successfully conceals a desire for self-justification. As Montaigne says, 'It is easier to accuse one sex than to excuse the other'. Sometimes what is going on is clear enough. For instance, the Roman law limiting the rights of woman cited 'the imbecility, the instability of the sex' just when the weakening of family ties seemed to threaten the interests of male heirs. And in the effort to keep the married woman under guardianship, appeal was made in the sixteenth century to the authority of St. Augustine, who declared that 'woman is a creature neither decisive nor constant', at a time when the single woman was thought capable of managing her property. Montaigne understood clearly how arbitrary and unjust was woman's appointed lot: 'Women are not in the wrong when they decline to accept the rules laid down for them, since the men make these rules without consulting them. No wonder intrigue and strife abound.' But he did not go so far as to champion their cause.

It was only later, in the eighteenth century, that genuinely democratic men began to view the matter objectively. Diderot, among others, strove to show that woman is, like man, a human being. Later John Stuart Mill came fervently to her defence. But these philosophers displayed unusual impartiality. In the nineteenth century the feminist quarrel became again a quarrel of partisans. One of the consequences of the industrial revolution was the entrance of women into productive labour, and it was just here that the claims of the feminists emerged from the realm of theory and acquired an economic basis, while their opponents became the more aggressive. Although landed property lost power to some extent, the bourgeoisie clung to the old morality that found the guarantee of private property in the solidity of the family. Woman was ordered back into the home the more harshly as her emancipation became a real menace. Even within the working class the men endeavoured to restrain woman's liberation, because they began to see the women as dangerous competitors—the more so because they were accustomed to work for lower wages.[1]

In proving woman's inferiority, the anti-feminists then began to draw not only upon religion, philosophy, and theology, as before, but also upon science—biology, experimental psychology, etc. At most they were willing to grant 'equality in difference' to the *other* sex. That profitable formula is most significant ; it is precisely like the 'equal but separate' formula of the Jim Crow laws aimed at the North American Negroes. As is well known, this so-called equalitarian segregation has resulted only in the most extreme discrimination. The similarity just noted is in no way due to chance, for whether it is a race, a caste, a class, or a sex that is reduced to a position of inferiority, the methods of justification are the same. 'The eternal feminine' corresponds to 'the black soul' and to 'the Jewish character'. True, the Jewish problem is on the whole very different from the other two—to the anti-Semite the Jew is not so much an inferior as he is an enemy for whom there is to be granted no place on earth, for whom annihilation is the fate desired. But there are deep similarities between the situation of woman and that of the Negro. Both are emancipated today from a like paternalism, and the former master class wishes

[1] See Part II, pp. 136-8.

15

to 'keep them in their place'—that is, the place chosen for them. In both cases the former masters lavish more or less sincere eulogies, either on the virtues of 'the good Negro' with his dormant, childish, merry soul—the submissive Negro —or on the merits of the woman who is 'truly feminine'— that is, frivolous, infantile, irresponsible—the submissive woman. In both cases the dominant class bases its argument on a state of affairs that it has itself created. As George Bernard Shaw puts it, in substance, 'The American white relegates the black to the rank of shoeshine boy; and he concludes from this that the black is good for nothing but shining shoes.' This vicious circle is met with in all analogous circumstances; when an individual (or a group of individuals) is kept in a situation of inferiority, the fact is that he *is* inferior. But the significance of the verb *to be* must be rightly understood here; it is in bad faith to give it a static value when it really has the dynamic Hegelian sense of 'to have become'. Yes, women on the whole *are* today inferior to men; that is, their situation affords them fewer possibilities. The question is: should that state of affairs continue?

Many men hope that it will continue; not all have given up the battle. The conservative bourgeoisie still see in the emancipation of women a menace to their morality and their interests. Some men dread feminine competition. Recently a male student wrote in the *Hebdo-Latin*: 'Every woman student who goes into medicine or law robs us of a job.' He never questioned his rights in this world. And economic interests are not the only ones concerned. One of the benefits that oppression confers upon the oppressors is that the most humble among them is made to *feel* superior; thus, a 'poor white' in the South can console himself with the thought that he is not a 'dirty nigger'—and the more prosperous whites cleverly exploit this pride.

Similarly, the most mediocre of males feels himself a demi-god as compared with women. It was much easier for M. de Montherlant to think himself a hero when he faced women (and women chosen for his purpose) than when he was obliged to act the man among men—something many women have done better than he, for that matter. And in September 1948, in one of his articles in the *Figaro littéraire*, Claude Mauriac—whose great originality is admired by all—could[1] write regarding woman: '*We* listen on a tone [*sic!*] of polite

[1] Or at least he thought he could.

indifference . . . to the most brilliant among them, well knowing that her wit reflects more or less luminously ideas that come from *us*.' Evidently the speaker referred to is not reflecting the ideas of Mauriac himself, for no one knows of his having any. It may be that she reflects ideas originating with men, but then, even among men there are those who have been known to appropriate ideas not their own ; and one can well ask whether Claude Mauriac might not find more interesting a conversation reflecting Descartes, Marx, or Gide rather than himself. What is really remarkable is that by using the questionable *we* he identifies himself with St. Paul, Hegel, Lenin, and Nietzsche, and from the lofty eminence of their grandeur looks disdainfully upon the bevy of women who make bold to converse with him on a footing of equality. In truth, I know of more than one woman who would refuse to suffer with patience Mauriac's 'tone of polite indifference.'

I have lingered on this example because the masculine attitude is here displayed with disarming ingenuousness. But men profit in more subtle ways from the otherness, the alterity of woman. Here is miraculous balm for those afflicted with an inferiority complex, and indeed no one is more arrogant towards women, more aggressive or scornful, than the man who is anxious about his virility. Those who are not fear-ridden in the presence of their fellow men are much more disposed to recognize a fellow creature in woman ; but even to these the myth of Woman, the Other, is precious for many reasons.[1] They cannot be blamed for not cheerfully relinquishing all the benefits they derive from the myth, for they realize what they would lose in relinquishing woman as they fancy her to be, while they fail to realize what they have to gain from the woman of tomorrow. Refusal to pose oneself as the Subject, unique and absolute, requires great self-denial. Furthermore, the vast majority of men make no such claim explicitly. They do not *postulate* woman as inferior, for today they are too thoroughly imbued with the

[1] A significant article on this theme by Michel Carrouges appears in No. 292 of the *Cahiers du Sud*. He writes indignantly: 'Would that there were no woman-myth at all but only a cohort of cooks, matrons, prostitutes, and bluestockings serving functions of pleasure or usefulness!' That is to say, in his view woman has no existence in and for herself; he thinks only of her *function* in the male world. Her reason for existence lies in man. But then, in fact, her poetic 'function' as a myth might be more valued than any other. The real problem is precisely to find out why woman should be defined with relation to man.

17

ideal of democracy not to recognize all human beings as equals.

In the bosom of the family, woman seems in the eyes of childhood and youth to be clothed in the same social dignity as the adult males. Later on, the young man, desiring and loving, experiences the resistance, the independence of the woman desired and loved; in marriage, he respects woman as wife and mother, and in the concrete events of conjugal life she stands there before him as a free being. He can therefore feel that social subordination as between the sexes no longer exists and that on the whole, in spite of differences, woman is an equal. As, however, he observes some points of inferiority—the most important being unfitness for the professions—he attributes these to natural causes. When he is in a co-operative and benevolent relation with woman, his theme is the principle of abstract equality, and he does not base his attitude upon such inequality as may exist. But when he is in conflict with her, the situation is reversed: his theme will be the existing inequality, and he will even take it as justification for denying abstract equality.

So it is that many men will affirm as if in good faith that women *are* the equals of man and that they have nothing to clamour for, while *at the same time* they will say that women can never be the equals of man and that their demands are in vain. It is, in point of fact, a difficult matter for man to realize the extreme importance of social discriminations which seem outwardly insignificant but which produce in woman moral and intellectual effects so profound that they appear to spring from her original nature.[1] The most sympathetic of men never fully comprehend woman's concrete situation. And there is no reason to put much trust in the men when they rush to the defence of privileges whose full extent they can hardly measure. We shall not, then, permit ourselves to be intimidated by the number and violence of the attacks launched against women, nor to be entrapped by the self-seeking eulogies bestowed on the 'true woman', nor to profit by the enthusiasm for woman's destiny manifested by men who would not for the world have any part of it.

We should consider the arguments of the feminists with no less suspicion, however, for very often their controversial aim deprives them of all real value. If the 'woman question'

[1] The specific purpose of Book Two of this study is to describe this process.

seems trivial, it is because masculine arrogance has made of it a 'quarrel'; and when quarrelling one no longer reasons well. People have tirelessly sought to prove that woman is superior, inferior, or equal to man. Some say that, having been created after Adam, she is evidently a secondary being; others say on the contrary that Adam was only a rough draft and that God succeeded in producing the human being in perfection when He created Eve. Woman's brain is smaller; yes, but it is relatively larger. Christ was made a man; yes, but perhaps for his greater humility. Each argument at once suggests its opposite, and both are often fallacious. If we are to gain understanding, we must get out of these ruts; we must discard the vague notions of superiority, inferiority, equality which have hitherto corrupted every discussion of the subject and start afresh.

Very well, but just how shall we pose the question? And, to begin with, who are we to propound it at all? Man is at once judge and party to the case; but so is woman. What we need is an angel—neither man nor woman—but where shall we find one? Still, the angel would be poorly qualified to speak, for an angel is ignorant of all the basic facts involved in the problem. With a hermaphrodite we should be no better off, for here the situation is most peculiar; the hermaphrodite is not really the combination of a whole man and a whole woman, but consists of parts of each and thus is neither. It looks to me as if there are, after all, certain women who are best qualified to elucidate the situation of woman. Let us not be misled by the sophism that because Epimenides was a Cretan he was necessarily a liar; it is not a mysterious essence that compels men and women to act in good or in bad faith, it is their situation that inclines them more or less towards the search for truth. Many of today's women, fortunate in the restoration of all the privileges pertaining to the estate of the human being, can afford the luxury of impartiality—we even recognize its necessity. We are no longer like our partisan elders; by and large we have won the game. In recent debates on the status of women the United Nations has persistently maintained that the equality of the sexes is now becoming a reality, and already some of us have never had to sense in our femininity an inconvenience or an obstacle. Many problems appear to us to be more pressing than those which concern us in particular, and this detachment even allows us to hope that our attitude will be objective. Still, we know the feminine
19

world more intimately than do the men because we have our roots in it, we grasp more immediately than do men what it means to a human being to be feminine; and we are more concerned with such knowledge. I have said that there are more pressing problems, but this does not prevent us from seeing some importance in asking how the fact of being women will affect our lives. What opportunities precisely have been given us and what withheld? What fate awaits our younger sisters, and what directions should they take? It is significant that books by women on women are in general animated in our day less by a wish to demand our rights than by an effort towards clarity and understanding. As we emerge from an era of excessive controversy, this book is offered as one attempt among others to confirm that statement.

But it is doubtless impossible to approach any human problems with a mind free from bias. The way in which questions are put, the points of view assumed, presuppose a relativity of interest; all characteristics imply values, and every objective description, so called, implies an ethical background. Rather than attempt to conceal principles more or less definitely implied, it is better to state them openly, at the beginning. This will make it unnecessary to specify on every page in just what sense one uses such words as *superior*, *inferior*, *better*, *worse*, *progress*, *reaction*, and the like. If we survey some of the works on woman, we note that one of the points of view most frequently adopted is that of the public good, the general interest; and one always means by this the benefit of society as one wishes it to be maintained or established. For our part, we hold that the only public good is that which assures the private good of the citizens; we shall pass judgment on institutions according to their effectiveness in giving concrete opportunities to individuals. But we do not confuse the idea of private interest with that of happiness, although that is another common point of view. Are not women of the harem more happy than women voters? Is not the housekeeper happier than the working-woman? It is not too clear just what the word *happy* really means and still less what true values it may mask. There is no possibility of measuring the happiness of others, and it is always easy to describe as happy the situation in which one wishes to place them.

In particular those who are condemned to stagnation are often pronounced happy on the pretext that happiness consists in being at rest. This notion we reject, for our perspective is that of existentialist ethics. Every subject plays his part as such specifically through exploits or projects that serve as a mode of transcendence; he achieves liberty only through a continual reaching out towards other liberties. There is no justification for present existence other than its expansion into an indefinitely open future. Every time transcendence falls back into immanence, stagnation, there is degradation of existence into the '*en-soi*'—the brutish life of subjection to given conditions—and of liberty into constraint and contingence. This downfall represents a moral fault if the subject consents to it; if it is inflicted upon him, it spells frustration and oppression. In both cases it is an absolute evil. Every individual concerned to justify his existence feels that his existence involves an undefined need to transcend himself, to engage in freely chosen projects.

Now, what peculiarly signalizes the situation of woman is that she—a free and autonomous being like all human creatures—nevertheless finds herself living in a world where men compel her to assume the status of the Other. They propose to stabilize her as object and to doom her to immanence since her transcendance is to be overshadowed and for ever transcended by another ego (*conscience*) which is essential and sovereign. The drama of woman lies in this conflict between the fundamental aspirations of every subject (ego)—who always regards the self as the essential—and the compulsions of a situation in which she is the inessential. How can a human being in woman's situation attain fulfilment? What roads are open to her? Which are blocked? How can independence be recovered in a state of dependency? What circumstances limit woman's liberty and how can they be overcome? These are the fundamental questions on which I would fain throw some light. This means that I am interested in the fortunes of the individual as defined not in terms of happiness but in terms of liberty.

Quite evidently this problem would be without significance if we were to believe that woman's destiny is inevitably determined by physiological, psychological, or economic forces. Hence I shall discuss first of all the light in which woman is viewed by biology, psychoanalysis, and historical materialism. Next I shall try to show exactly how the concept of the 'truly feminine' has been fashioned—why woman has been defined as the Other—and what have been the consequences from man's point of view. Then from woman's point of view I shall describe the world in which women must live ; and thus we shall be able to envisage the difficulties in their way as, endeavouring to make their escape from the sphere hitherto assigned them, they aspire to full membership in the human race.

PART I

DESTINY

CHAPTER I

THE DATA OF BIOLOGY

WOMAN? Very simple, say the fanciers of simple formulas: she is a womb, an ovary; she is a female—this word is sufficient to define her. In the mouth of a man the epithet *female* has the sound of an insult, yet he is not ashamed of his animal nature; on the contrary, he is proud if someone says of him: 'He is a male!' The term 'female' is derogatory not because it emphasizes woman's animality, but because it imprisons her in her sex; and if this sex seems to man to be contemptible and inimical even in harmless dumb animals, it is evidently because of the uneasy hostility stirred up in him by woman. Nevertheless he wishes to find in biology a justification for this sentiment. The word *female* brings up in his mind a saraband of imagery—a vast, round ovum engulfs and castrates the agile spermatozoon; the monstrous and swollen termite queen rules over the enslaved males; the female praying mantis and the spider, satiated with love, crush and devour their partners; the bitch in heat runs through the alleys, trailing behind her a wake of depraved odours; the she-monkey presents her posterior immodestly and then steals away with hypocritical coquetry; and the most superb wild beasts—the tigress, the lioness, the panther—bed down slavishly under the imperial embrace of the male. Females sluggish, eager, artful, stupid, callous, lustful, ferocious, abased—man projects them all at once upon woman. And the fact is that she is a female. But if we are willing to stop thinking in platitudes, two questions are immediately posed: what does the female denote in the animal kingdom? And what particular kind of female is manifest in woman?

Males and females are two types of individuals which are differentiated within a species for the function of reproduction; they can be defined only correlatively. But first it must be noted that even the *division* of a species into two sexes is not always clear-cut.

In nature it is not universally manifested. To speak only of animals, it is well known that among the microscopic one-celled forms—infusoria, amoebae, sporozoans, and the like—multiplication is fundamentally distinct from sexuality. Each cell divides and subdivides by itself. In many-celled animals or metazoans reproduction may take place asexually, either by schizogenesis—that is, by fission or cutting into two or more parts which become new individuals—or by blastogenesis—that is, by buds that separate and form new individuals. The phenomena of budding observed in the fresh-water hydra and other coelenterates, in sponges, worms, and tunicates, are well-known examples. In cases of parthenogenesis the egg of the virgin female develops into an embryo without fertilization by the male, which thus may play no role at all. In the honey-bee copulation takes place, but the eggs may or may not be fertilized at the time of laying. The unfertilized eggs undergo development and produce the drones (males); in the aphids males are absent during a series of generations in which the eggs are unfertilized and produce females. Parthenogenesis has been induced artificially in the sea urchin, the starfish, the frog, and other species. Among the one-celled animals (Protozoa), however, two cells may fuse, forming what is called a zygote; and in the honey-bee fertilization is necessary if the eggs are to produce females. In the aphids both males and females appear in the autumn, and the fertilized eggs then produced are adapted for overwintering.

Certain biologists in the past concluded from these facts that even in species capable of asexual propagation occasional fertilization is necessary to renew the vigour of the race—to accomplish 'rejuvenation'—through the mixing of hereditary material from two individuals. On this hypothesis sexuality might well appear to be an indispensable function in the most complex forms of life; only the lower organisms could multiply without sexuality; and even here vitality would after a time become exhausted. But today this hypothesis is largely abandoned; research has proved that under suitable conditions asexual multiplication can go on indefinitely without noticeable degeneration, a fact that is especially striking in the bacteria and Protozoa. More and more numerous and daring experiments in parthenogenesis are being performed, and in many species the male appears to be funda-

mentally unnecessary. Besides, if the value of intercellular exchange were demonstrated, that value would seem to stand as
a sheer, unexplained fact. Biology certainly demonstrates the
existence of sexual differentiation, but from the point of
view of any end to be attained the science could not infer
such differentiation from the structure of the cell, nor from
the laws of cellular multiplication, nor from any basic
phenomenon.[1]

The production of two types of gametes, the sperm and
the egg, does not necessarily imply the existence of two
distinct sexes; as a matter of fact, egg and sperm—two
highly differentiated types of reproductive cells—may both
be produced by the same individual. This occurs in normally
hermaphroditic species, which are common among plants
and are also to be found among the lower animals, such
as annelid worms and molluscs. In them reproduction may
be accomplished through self-fertilization or, more commonly,
cross-fertilization. Here again certain biologists have attempted to account for the existing state of affairs. Some
hold that the separation of the gonads (ovaries and testes)
in two distinct individuals represent an evolutionary advance
over hermaphroditism; others on the contrary regard the
separate condition as primitive, and believe that hermaphroditism represents a degenerate state. These notions
regarding the superiority of one system or the other imply
the most debatable evolutionary theorizing. All that we can
say for sure is that these two modes of reproduction co-
exist in nature, that they both succeed in accomplishing the
survival of the species concerned, and that the differentiation
of the gametes, like that of the organisms producing them,
appears to be accidental. It would seem, then, that the
division of a species into male and female individuals is
simply an irreducible fact of observation.

In most philosophies this fact has been taken for granted
without pretence of explanation. According to the Platonic
myth, there were at the beginning men, women, and herma-
phrodites. Each individual had two faces, four arms, four
legs, and two conjoined bodies. At a certain time they were
split in two, and ever since each half seeks to rejoin its

[1] In modern evolutionary theory, however, the mixing of hereditary factors (genes) brought about by sexual reproduction is
considered highly important since it affords a constant supply of
new combinations for natural selection to act upon. And sexual
differentiation often plays an important part in sexual reproduction.—Tr.

corresponding half. Later the gods decreed that new human beings should be created through the coupling of dissimilar halves. But it is only love that this story is intended to explain; division into sexes is assumed at the outset. Nor does Aristotle explain this division, for if matter and form must co-operate in all action, there is no necessity for the active and passive principles to be separated in two different categories of individuals. Thus St. Thomas proclaims woman an 'incidental' being, which is a way of suggesting—from the male point of view—the accidental or contingent nature of sexuality. Hegel, however, would have been untrue to his passion for rationalism had he failed to attempt a logical explanation. Sexuality in his view represents the medium through which the subject attains a concrete sense of belonging to a particular kind (*genre*). 'The sense of kind is produced in the subject as an effect which offsets this disproportionate sense of his individual reality, as a desire to find the sense of himself in another individual of his species through union with this other, to complete himself and thus to incorporate the kind (*genre*) within his own nature and bring it into existence. This is copulation' (*Philosophy of Nature*, Part 3, Section 369). And a little farther on: 'The process consists in this, namely: that which they are in themselves, that is to say a single kind, one and the same subjective life, they also establish it as such.' And Hegel states later that for the uniting process to be accomplished, there must first be sexual differentiation. But his exposition is not convincing: one feels in it all too distinctly the predetermination to find in every operation the three terms of the syllogism.

The projection or transcendence of the individual towards the species, in which both individual and species are fulfilled, could be accomplished without the intervention of a third element in the simple relation of progenitor to offspring; that is to say, reproduction could be asexual. Or, if there were to be two progenitors, they could be similar (as happens in hermaphroditic species) and differentiated only as particular individuals of a single type. Hegel's discussion reveals a most important significance of sexuality, but his mistake is always to argue from significance to necessity, to equate significance with necessity. Man gives significance to the sexes and their relations through sexual activity, just as he gives sense and value to all the functions that he exercises; but sexual activity is not necessarily implied in the nature of the human being. Merleau-Ponty notes in the *Phénoménologie de la perception* that human existence requires us to revise our ideas of necessity and contingency. 'Existence,' he says, 'has no casual, fortuitous qualities, no content that does not contribute to the formation of its aspect; it does not admit the notion of sheer fact, for it is only through existence that the facts are manifested.' True enough. But it is also true that there are conditions without which the very fact of existence itself would seem to be impossible. To be present in the world implies strictly that there exists a body which is at once a material thing in the world and a point of view towards this world; but nothing requires that this body have this or that particular structure. Sartre discusses in *L'Etre et le néant* Heidegger's dictum to the effect that the real nature of man is bound up with death because of man's finite state. He shows that an existence which is finite and yet unlimited in time is conceivable; but none the less if death were not resident in human life, the relation of man to the world and to himself would be profoundly disarranged—so much so that the statement 'Man is mortal' would be seen to have significance quite other than that of a mere fact of observation. Were he immortal, an existent would no longer be what we call a man. One of the essential features of his career is that the progress of his life through time creates behind him and before him the infinite past and future, and it would seem, then, that the perpetuation of the species is the correlative of his individual limitation. Thus we can regard the phenomenon of reproduction as founded in the very nature of being. But we must stop there. The perpetuation of the species does not necessitate sexual differentiation. True enough, this differentiation is characteristic of existents to such an extent that it belongs in any realistic definition of existence. But it nevertheless remains true that both a mind without a body and an immortal man are strictly inconceivable, whereas we can imagine a parthenogenetic or hermaphroditic society.

On the respective functions of the two sexes man has entertained a great variety of beliefs. At first they had no scientific basis, simply reflecting social myths. It was long thought—and it is still believed in certain primitive matriarchal societies—that the father plays no part in conception. Ancestral spirits in the form of living germs are supposed to find their way into the maternal body. With the advent of patriarchal institutions, the male laid eager claim to his posterity. It was still necessary to grant the mother a part in procreation, but it was conceded only that she carried and nourished the living seed, created by the father alone. Aristotle fancied that the fetus arose from the union of sperm and menstrual blood, woman furnishing only passive matter while the male principle contributed force, activity, movement, life. Hippocrates held to a similar doctrine, recognizing two kinds of seed, the weak or female and the strong or male. The theory of Aristotle survived through the Middle Ages and into modern times.

At the end of the seventeenth century Harvey killed female dogs shortly after copulation and found in the horns of the uterus small sacs that he thought were eggs but that were really embryos. The Danish anatomist Steno gave the name of ovaries to the female genital glands, previously called 'feminine testicles', and noted on their surface the small swellings that von Graaf in 1677 erroneously identified with the eggs and that are now called Graafian follicles. The ovary was still regarded as homologous to the male gland. In the same year, however, the 'spermatic animalcules' were discovered and it was proved that they penetrated into the uterus of the female; but it was supposed that they were simply nourished therein and that the coming individual was preformed in them. In 1694 a Dutchman, Hartsaker, drew a picture of the 'homunculus' hidden in the spermatozoon, and in 1699, another scientist said that he had seen the spermatozoon cast off a kind of moult under which appeared a little man, which he also drew. Under these imaginative hypotheses, woman was restricted to the nourishment of an active, living principle already preformed in perfection. These notions were not universally accepted, and they were argued into the nineteenth century. The use of the microscope enabled von Baer in 1827 to discover the mammalian egg, contained inside the Graafian follicle. Before long it was possible to study the cleavage of the egg—that is, the early stage of development through cell division—and in 1835 sarcode, later called protoplasm, was discovered and the true nature of the cell began to be realized. In 1879 the penetration of the spermatozoon into the starfish egg was observed, and thereupon the equivalence of the nuclei of the two gametes, egg and sperm, was established. The details of their union within the fertilized egg were first worked out in 1883 by a Belgian zoologist, van Beneden.

Aristotle's ideas were not wholly discredited, however. Hegel held that the two sexes were of necessity different, the one active and the other passive, and of course the female would be the passive one. 'Thus man, in consequence of that differentiation, is the active principle while woman is the passive principle because she remains undeveloped in her unity.'[1] And even after the egg had been recognized as an active principle, men still tried to make a point of its quiescence as contrasted with the lively movements of the sperm. Today one notes an opposite tendency on the part of some scientists. The discoveries made in the course of experiments on parthenogenesis have led them to reduce the function of the sperm to that of a simple physicochemical reagent. It has been shown that in certain species the stimulus of an acid or even of a needle-prick is enough to initiate the cleavage of the egg and the development of the embryo. On this basis it has been boldly suggested that the male gamete (sperm) is not necessary for reproduction, that it acts at most as a ferment; further, that perhaps in time the co-operation of the male will become unnecessary in procreation—the answer, it would seem, to many a woman's prayer. But there is no warrant for so bold an expectation, for nothing warrants us in universalizing specific life processes. The phenomena of asexual propogation and of parthenogenesis appear to be neither more nor less fundamental than those of sexual reproduction. I have said that the latter has no claim *a priori* to be considered basic; but neither does any fact indicate that it is reducible to any more fundamental mechanism.

Thus, admitting no *a priori* doctrine, no dubious theory, we are confronted by a fact for which we can offer no basis in the nature of things nor any explanation through observed data, and the significance of which we cannot comprehend *a priori*. We can hope to grasp the significance of sexuality only by studying it in its concrete manifestations; and then perhaps the meaning of the word *female* will stand revealed.

I do not intend to offer here a philosophy of life; and I do not care to take sides prematurely in the dispute between the mechanistic and the purposive or teleological philosophies. It is to be noted, however, that all physiologists and biologists use more or less finalistic language, if only because they ascribe meaning to vital phenomena. I shall adopt their

[1] HEGEL, *Philosophy of Nature.*

31

terminology. Without taking any stand on the relation between life and consciousness, we can assert that every biological fact implies transcendence, that every function involves a project, something to be done. Let my words be taken to imply no more than that.

In the vast majority of species male and female individuals co-operate in reproduction. They are defined primarily as male and female by the gametes which they produce—sperms and eggs respectively. In some lower plants and animals the cells that fuse to form the zygote are identical; and these cases of isogamy are significant because they illustrate the basic equivalence of the gametes.[1] In general the gametes are differentiated, and yet their equivalence remains a striking fact. Sperms and eggs develop from similar primordial germ cells in the two sexes. The development of oocytes from the primordial cells in the female differs from that of spermatocytes in the male chiefly in regard to the protoplasm, but the nuclear phenomena are clearly the same. The biologist Ancel suggested in 1903 that the primordial germ cell is indifferent and undergoes development into sperm or egg depending upon which type of gonad, testis or ovary, contains it. However this may be, the primordial germ cells of each sex contain the same number of chromosomes (that characteristic of the species concerned), which number is reduced to one half by closely analogous process in male and female. At the end of these developmental processes (called spermatogenesis in the male and oogenesis in the female) the gametes appear fully matured as sperms and eggs, differing enormously in some respects, as noted below, but being alike in that each contains a single set of equivalent chromosomes.

Today it is well known that the sex of offspring is determined by the chromosome constitution established at the time of fertilization. According to the species concerned, it is either the male gamete or the female gamete that accom-

[1] Isogamous gametes are identical in appearance, but in some cases (certain fungi and protozoans) experiment has shown conclusively that invisible physiological differences exist, for two gametes will not fuse unless they come from different strains of the species. Here may be traced a sexual differentiation more fundamental than that of egg and sperm or male and female organism. As the author says, the gametes are equivalent; but it may well be that they are never absolutely identical, as the term *isogamy* implies.—TR.

plishes this result. In the mammals it is the sperm, of which two kinds are produced in equal numbers, one kind containing an X-chromosome (as do all the eggs), the other kind containing a Y-chromosome (not found in the eggs). Aside from the X- and Y-chromosomes, egg and sperm contain an equivalent set of these bodies. It is obvious that when sperm and egg unite in fertilization, the fertilized egg will contain two full sets of chromosomes, making up the number characteristic of the species—48 in man, for example. If fertilization is accomplished by an X-bearing sperm, the fertilized egg will contain two X-chromosomes and will develop into a female (XX). If the Y-bearing sperm fertilizes the egg, only one X-chromosome will be present and the sex will be male (XY). In birds and butterflies the situation is reversed, though the principle remains the same ; it is the eggs that contain either X or Y and hence determine the sex of the offspring. In the matter of heredity, the laws of Mendel show that the father and the mother play equal parts. The chromosomes contain the factors of heredity (genes), and they are conveyed equally in egg and sperm.

What we should note in particular at this point is that neither gamete can be regarded as superior to the other ; when they unite, both lose their individuality in the fertilized egg. There are two common suppositions which—at least on this basic biological level—are clearly false. The first—that of the passivity of the female—is disproved by the fact that new life springs from the union of the two gametes ; the living spark is not the exclusive property of either. The nucleus of the egg is a centre of vital activity exactly symmetrical with the nucleus of the sperm. The second false supposition contradicts the first—which does not seem to prevent their coexistence. It is to the effect that the permanence of the species is assured by the female, the male principle being of an explosive and transitory nature. As a matter of fact, the embryo carries on the germ plasm of the father as well as that of the mother, and transmits them together to its descendants under now male, now female form. It is, so to speak, an androgynous germ plasm, which outlives the male or female individuals that are its incarnations, whenever they produce offspring.

This said, we can turn our attention to secondary differences between egg and sperm, which are of the greatest interest. The essential peculiarity of the egg is that it is provided with means for nourishing and protecting the embryo ;

33

it stores up reserve material from which the fetus will build its tissues, material that is not living substance but inert yolk. In consequence the egg is of massive, commonly spherical form and relatively large. The size of birds' eggs is well known; in woman the egg is almost microscopic, about equal in size to a printed period (diameter .132-.135 mm.), but the human sperm is far smaller (.04-.06 mm. in length), so small that a cubic millimetre would hold 60,000. The sperm has a threadlike tail and a small, flattened oval head, which contains the chromosomes. No inert substance weighs it down; it is wholly alive. In its whole structure it is adapted for mobility. Whereas the egg, big with the future of the embryo, is stationary; enclosed within the female body or floating externally in water, it passively awaits fertilization. It is the male gamete that seeks it out. The sperm is always a naked cell; the egg may or may not be protected with shell and membranes according to the species; but in any case, when the sperm makes contact with the egg, it presses against it, sometimes shakes it, and bores into it. The tail is dropped and the head enlarges, forming the male nucleus, which now moves towards the egg nucleus. Meanwhile the egg quickly forms a membrane, which prevents the entrance of other sperms. In the starfish and other echinoderms, where fertilization takes place externally, it is easy to observe the onslaught of the sperms, which surround the egg like an aureole. The competition involved is an important phenomenon, and it occurs in most species. Being much smaller than the egg, the sperm is generally produced in far greater numbers (more than 200,000,000 to 1 in the human species), and so each egg has numerous suitors.

Thus the egg—active in its essential feature, the nucleus—is superficially passive; its compact mass, sealed up within itself, evokes nocturnal darkness and inward repose. It was the form of the sphere that to the ancients represented the circumscribed world, the impenetrable atom. Motionless, the egg waits; in contrast the sperm—free, slender, agile—typifies the impatience and the restlessness of existence. But allegory should not be pushed too far. The ovule has sometimes been likened to immanence, the sperm to transcendence, and it has been said that the sperm penetrates the female element only in losing its transcendence, its motility; it is seized and castrated by the inert mass that engulfs it after depriving it of its tail. This is magical action—disquieting, as is all passive

34

action—whereas the activity of the male gamete is rational; it is movement measurable in terms of time and space. The truth is that these notions are hardly more than vagaries of the mind. Male and female gametes fuse in the fertilized egg; they are both suppressed in becoming a new whole. It is false to say that the egg greedily swallows the sperm, and equally so to say that the sperm victoriously commandeers the female cell's reserves, since in the act of fusion the individuality of both is lost. No doubt movement seems to the mechanistic mind to be an eminently rational phenomenon, but it is an idea no clearer for modern physics than action at a distance. Besides, we do not know in detail the physicochemical reactions that lead up to gametic union. We can derive a valid suggestion, however, from this comparison of the gametes. There are two interrelated dynamic aspects of life: it can be maintained only through transcending itself, and it can transcend itself only on condition that it is maintained. These two factors always operate together and it is unrealistic to try to separate them, yet now it is one and now the other that dominates. The two gametes at once transcend and perpetuate themselves when they unite; but in its structure the egg anticipates future needs, it is so constituted as to nourish the life that will wake within it. The sperm, on the contrary, is in no way equipped to provide for the development of the embryo it awakens. On the other hand, the egg cannot provide the change of environment that will stimulate a new outburst of life, whereas the sperm can and does travel. Without the foresight of the egg, the sperm's arrival would be in vain; but without the initiative of the latter, the egg would not fulfil its living potentialities.

We may conclude, then, that the two gametes play a fundamentally identical role; together they create a living being in which both of them are at once lost and transcended. But in the secondary and superficial phenomena upon which fertilization depends, it is the male element which provides the stimuli needed for evoking new life and it is the female element that enables this new life to be lodged in a stable organism.

It would be foolhardy indeed to deduce from such evidence that woman's place is in the home—but there are foolhardy men. In his book *Le Tempérament et le charactère*, Alfred Fouillée undertakes to found his definition of woman *in toto* upon the egg and that of man upon the spermatozoon; and a number of supposedly profound theories rest upon this play of doubtful analogies. It is a question to what philosophy of nature these dubious ideas pertain; not to the laws of heredity, certainly, for according to these laws, men and women alike develop from an egg and a sperm. I can only suppose that in such misty minds there still float shreds of the old philosophy of the Middle Ages which taught that the cosmos is an exact reflection of a microcosm—the egg is imagined to be a little female, the woman a giant egg. These musings, generally abandoned since the days of alchemy, make a bizarre contrast with the scientific precision of the data upon which they are now based, for modern biology conforms with difficulty to medieval symbolism. But our theorizers do not look too closely into the matter. In all honesty it must be admitted that in any case it is a long way from the egg to woman. In the unfertilized egg not even the concept of femaleness is as yet established. As Hegel justly remarks, the sexual relation cannot be referred back to the relation of the gametes. It is our duty, then, to study the female organism as a whole.

It has already been pointed out that in many plants and in some animals (such as snails) the presence of two kinds of gametes does not require two kinds of individuals, since every individual produces both eggs and sperms. Even when the sexes are separate, they are not distinguished in any such fashion as are different species. Males and females appear rather to be variations on a common groundwork, much as the two gametes are differentiated from similar original tissue. In certain animals (for example, the marine worm *Bonellia*) the larva is asexual, the adult becoming male or female according to the circumstances under which it has developed. But as noted above (page 31), sex is determined in most species by the genotypic constitution of the fertilized egg. In bees the unfertilized eggs laid by the queen produce males exclusively; in aphids parthenogenetic eggs usually produce females. But in most animals all eggs that develop have been fertilized, and it is notable that the sexes are produced in approximately equal numbers through the mechanism of chromosomal sex-determination, already explained.

In the embryonic development of both sexes the tissue from which the gonads will be formed is at first indifferent; at a certain stage either testes or ovaries become established; and similarly in the development of the other sex organs there is an early indifferent period when the sex of the

36

embryo cannot be told from an examination of these parts, from which, later on, the definitive male or female structures arise. All this helps to explain the existence of conditions intermediate between hermaphroditism and gonochorism (sexes separate). Very often one sex possesses certain organs characteristic of the other; a case in point is the toad, in which there is in the male a rudimentary ovary called Bidder's organ, capable of producing eggs under experimental conditions. Among the mammals there are indications of this sexual bipotentiality, such as the *uterus masculinus* and the rudimentary mammary glands in the male, and in the female Gärtner's canal and the clitoris. Even in those species exhibiting a high degree of sexual differentiation individuals combining both male and female characteristics may occur. Many cases of intersexuality are known in both animals and man; and among insects and crustaceans one occasionally finds examples of gynandromorphism, in which male and female areas of the body are mingled in a kind of mosaic.

The fact is that the individual, though its genotypic sex is fixed at fertilization, can be profoundly affected by the environment in which it develops. In the ants, bees, and termites the larval nutrition determines whether the genotypic female individual will become a fully developed female ('queen') or a sexually retarded worker. In these cases the whole organism is affected; but the gonads do not play a part in establishing the sexual differences of the body, or *soma*. In the vertebrates, however, the hormones secreted by the gonads are the essential regulators. Numerous experiments show that by varying the hormonal (endocrine) situation, sex can be profoundly affected. Grafting and castration experiments on adult animals and man have contributed to the modern theory of sexuality, according to which the soma is in a way identical in male and female vertebrates. It may be regarded as a kind of neutral element upon which the influence of the gonad imposes the sexual characteristics.[1] Some of the hormones secreted by the gonad act as stimulators, others as inhibitors. Even the genital tract itself is somatic, and embryological investigations show that it develops in the male or female direction from an indifferent and

[1] In connection with this view, it must be remembered that in man and many animals the soma is not strictly neutral, since all its cells are genotypically either male (XY) or female (XX). This is why the young individual normally produces either the male or the female hormonal environment, leading normally to the development of either male or female characteristics.—Tr.

37

in some respects hermaphroditic condition under the hormonal influence. Intersexuality may result when the hormones are abnormal and hence neither one of the two sexual potentialities is exclusively realized.

Numerically equal in the species and developed similarly from like beginnings, the fully formed male and female are basically equivalent. Both have reproductive glands—ovaries or testes—in which the gametes are produced by strictly corresponding processes, as we have seen. These glands discharge their products through ducts that are more or less complex according to sex ; in the female the egg may pass directly to the outside through the oviduct, or it may be retained for a time in the cloaca or the uterus before expulsion ; in the male the semen may be deposited outside, or there may be a copulatory organ through which it is introduced into the body of the female. In these respects, then, male and female appear to stand in a symmetrical relation to each other. To reveal their peculiar, specific qualities it will be necessary to study them from the functional point of view.

It is extremely difficult to give a generally valid definition of the female. To define her as the bearer of the eggs and the male as bearer of the sperms is far from sufficient, since the relation of the organism to the gonads is, as we have seen, quite variable. On the other hand, the differences between the gametes have no direct effect upon the organism as a whole ; it has sometimes been argued that the eggs, being large, consume more vital energy than do the sperms, but the latter are produced in such infinitely greater numbers that the expenditure of energy must be about equal in the two sexes. Some have wished to see in spermatogenesis an example of prodigality and in oogenesis a model of economy, but there is an absurd liberality in the latter, too, for the vast majority of eggs are never fertilized.[1] In no way do gametes and gonads represent in microcosm the organism as a whole. It is to this—the whole organism—that we must now direct our attention.

One of the most remarkable features to be noted as we survey the scale of animal life is that as we go up, individuality is seen to be more and more fully developed. At the bottom, life is concerned only in the survival of the species

[1] For example, a woman produces about 400 eggs and at most 25 or 30 children; in animals the disproportion is often much greater.—Tr.

as a whole; at the top, life seeks expression through particular individuals, while accomplishing also the survival of the group. In some lower species the organism may be almost entirely reduced to the reproductive apparatus; in this case the egg, and hence the female, is supreme, since the egg is especially dedicated to the mere propagation of life; but here the female is hardly more than an abdomen, and her existence is entirely used up in a monstrous travail of ovulation. In comparison with the male, she reaches giant proportions; but her appendages are often tiny, her body a shapeless sac, her organs degenerated in favour of the eggs. Indeed, such males and females, although they are distinct organisms, can hardly be regarded as individuals, for they form a kind of unity made up of inseparable elements. In a way they are intermediate between hermaphroditism and gonochorism.

Thus in certain Crustacea, parasitic on the crab, the female is a mere sac enclosing millions of eggs, among which are found the minute males, both larval and adult. In *Edriolydnus* the dwarf male is still more degenerate; it lives under the shell of the female and has no digestive tract of its own, being purely reproductive in function. But in all such cases the female is no less restricted than the male; it is enslaved to the species. If the male is bound to the female, the latter is no less bound down, either to a living organism on which it exists as a parasite or to some substratum; and its substance is consumed in producing eggs which the tiny male fertilizes.

Among somewhat higher animals an individual autonomy begins to be manifested and the bond that joins the sexes weakens; but in the insects they both remain strictly subordinated to the eggs. Frequently, as in the mayflies, male and female die immediately after copulation and egg-laying. In some rotifers the male lacks a digestive tract and dies after fecundation; the female is able to eat and survives long enough at least to develop and lay the eggs. The mother dies after the appearance of the next generation is assured. The privileged position held by the females in many insects comes from the fact that the production and sometimes the care of the eggs demand a long effort, whereas fecundation is for the most part quickly accomplished.

In the termites the enormous queen, crammed with nourishment and laying as many as 4000 eggs per day until she becomes sterile and is pitilessly killed, is no less a slave than the comparatively tiny male who attends her and provides frequent fecundations. In the matriarchal ants' nests and beehives the males are economically useless and are killed off at times. At the season of the nuptial flight in ants, all the males emerge with females from the nest; those that succeed in mating with females die at once, exhausted; the rest are not permitted by the workers to re-enter the nest, and die of hunger or are killed. The fertilized female has a gloomy fate; she buries herself alone in the ground and often dies while laying her first eggs, or if she succeeds in founding a colony she remains shut in and may live for ten or twelve years constantly producing more eggs. The workers, females with atrophied sexuality, may live for several years, but their life is largely devoted to raising the larvae. It is much the same with bees; the drone that succeeds in mating with the queen during the nuptial flight falls to earth disembowelled; the other drones return to the hive, where they live a lazy life and are in the way until at the approach of winter they are killed off by the workers. But the workers purchase their right to live by incessant toil; as in the ants they are undeveloped females. The queen is in truth enslaved to the hive, laying eggs continually. If she dies, the workers give several larvae special food so as to provide for the succession; the first to emerge kills the rest in their cells.

In certain spiders the female carries the eggs about with her in a silken case until they hatch. She is much larger and stronger than the male and may kill and devour him after copulation, as does an insect, the praying mantis, around which has crystallized the myth of devouring femininity—the egg castrates the sperm, the mantis murders her spouse, these acts foreshadowing a feminine dream of castration. The mantis, however, shows her cruelty especially in captivity; and under natural conditions, when she is free in the midst of abundant food, she rarely dines on the male. If she does eat him, it is to enable her to produce her eggs and thus perpetuate the race, just as the solitary fertilized ant often eats some of her own eggs under the same necessity. It is going far afield to see in these facts a proclamation of the 'battle of the sexes' which sets individuals, as such, one against another. It cannot simply be said that in ants, bees, termites, spiders, or mantises the female enslaves and sometimes devours the male, for it is the species that in different ways consumes them both. The female lives longer and seems to be more important than the male; but she has no independence—egg-laying and the care of eggs and larvae

40

are her destiny, other functions being atrophied wholly or in part.

In the male, on the contrary, an individual existence begins to be manifested. In impregnation he very often shows more initiative than the female, seeking her out, making the approach, palpating, seizing, and forcing connection upon her. Sometimes he has to battle for her with other males. Accordingly the organs of locomotion, touch, and prehension are frequently more highly evolved in the male. Many female moths are wingless, while the males have wings; and often the males of insects have more highly developed colours, wing-covers, legs, and pincers. And sometimes to this endowment is added a seeming luxury of brilliant coloration. Beyond the brief moment of copulation the life of the male is useless and irresponsible; compared with the industriousness of the workers, the idleness of the drones seems a remarkable privilege. But this privilege is a social disgrace, and often the male pays with his life for his futility and partial independence. The species, which holds the female in slavery, punishes the male for his gesture towards escape; it liquidates him with brutal force.

In higher forms of life, reproduction becomes the creation of discrete organisms; it takes on a double role: maintenance of the species and creation of new individuals. This innovating aspect becomes the more unmistakable as the singularity of the individual becomes pronounced. It is striking then that these two essential elements—perpetuation and creation—are separately apportioned to the two sexes. This separation, already indicated at the moment when the egg is fertilized, is to be discerned in the whole generative process. It is not the essential nature of the egg that requires this separation, for in higher forms of life the female has, like the male, attained certain autonomy and her bondage to the egg has been relaxed. The female fish, batracian, or bird is far from being a mere abdomen. The less strictly the mother is bound to the egg, the less does the labour of reproduction represent an absorbing task and the more uncertainty there is in the relations of the two parents with their offspring. It can even happen that the father will take charge of the newly hatched young, as in various fishes.

Water is an element in which the eggs and sperms can float about and unite, and fecundation in the aquatic environment is most always external. Most fish do not copulate, at most stimulating one another by contact. The mother discharges the eggs, the father the sperm—their role is identical. There is no reason why the mother, any more than the father, should feel responsibility for the eggs. In some species the eggs are abandoned by the parents and develop without assistance ; sometimes a nest is prepared by the mother and sometimes she watches over the eggs after they have been fertilized. But very often it is the father who takes charge of them. As soon as he has fertilized them, he drives away the female to prevent her from eating them, and he protects them savagely against any intruder. Certain males have been described as making a kind of protective nest by blowing bubbles of air enclosed in an insulating substance ; and in many cases they protect the developing eggs in their mouths or, as in the seahorse, in abdominal folds.

In the batrachians (frogs and toads) similar phenomena are to be seen. True copulation is unknown to them ; they practise amplexus, the male embracing the female and thus stimulating her to lay her eggs. As the eggs are discharged, the sperms are deposited upon them. In the obstetrical toad the male wraps the strings of eggs about his hind legs and protects them, taking them into the water when the young are about to hatch as tadpoles.

In birds the egg is formed rather slowly inside the female ; it is relatively large and is laid with some difficulty. It is much more closely associated with the mother than with the father, who has simply fertilized it in a brief copulation. Usually the mother sits on the eggs and takes care of the newly hatched young ; but often the father helps in nest-building and in the protection and feeding of the young birds. In rare cases—for example, among the sparrows—the male does the incubating and rearing. Male and female pigeons secrete in the crop a milky fluid with which they both feed the fledglings. It is remarkable that in these cases where the male takes part in nourishing the young, there is no production of sperms during the time devoted to them— while occupied in maintaining life the male has no urge to beget new living beings.

In the mammals life assumes the most complex forms, and individualization is most advanced and specific. There the division of the two vital components—maintenance and creation—is realized definitively in the separation of the sexes. It is in this group that the mother sustains the closest relations—among vertebrates—with her offspring, and the father shows less interest in them. The female organism is wholly adapted for and subservient to maternity, while sexual initiative is the prerogative of the male.

The female is the victim of the species. During certain periods in the year, fixed in each species, her whole life is under the regulation of a sexual cycle (the oestrus cycle), of which the duration, as well as the rhythmic sequence of events, varies from one species to another. This cycle consists of two phases: during the first phase the eggs (variable in number according to the species) become mature and the lining of the uterus becomes thickened and vascular ; during the second phase (if fertilization has not occurred) the egg disappears, the uterine edifice breaks down, and the material is eliminated in a more or less noticeable temporary flow, known as menstruation in woman and related higher mammals. If fertilization does occur, the second phase is replaced by pregnancy. The time of ovulation (at the end of the first phase) is known as *oestrus* and it corresponds to the period of rut, heat, or sexual activity.

In the female mammal, rut is largely passive ; she is ready and waiting to receive the male. It may happen in mammals —as in certain birds—that she solicits the male, but she does no more than appeal to him by means of cries, displays, and suggestive attitudinizing. She is quite unable to force copulation upon him. In the end it is he who makes the decision. We have seen that even in the insects, where the female is highly privileged in return for her total sacrifice to the species, it is usually the male who takes the initiative in fecundation ; among the fishes he often stimulates the female to lay her eggs through his presence and contact ; and in the frogs and toads he acts as a stimulator in amplexus. But it is in birds and mammals especially that he forces himself upon her, while very often she submits indifferently or even resists him.

Even when she is willing, or provocative, it is unquestionably the male who *takes* the female—she is *taken*. Often the word applies literally, for whether by means of special organs or through superior strength, the male seizes her and holds her in place ; he performs the copulatory movements ; and, among insects, birds, and mammals, he penetrates her. In this penetration her inwardness is violated, she is like an enclosure that is broken into. The male is not doing violence to the species, for the species survives only in being constantly renewed and would come to an end if eggs and sperms did not come together ; but the female, entrusted

43

with the protection of the egg, locks it away inside herself, and her body, in sheltering the egg, shields it also from the fecundating action of the male. Her body becomes, therefore, a resistance to be broken through, whereas in penetrating it the male finds self-fulfilment in activity.

His domination is expressed in the very posture of copulation—in almost all animals the male is *on* the female. And certainly the organ he uses is a material object, but it appears here in its animated state—it is a tool—whereas in this performance the female organ is more in the nature of an inert receptacle. The male deposits his semen, the female receives it. Thus, though the female plays a fundamentally active role in procreation, she *submits to* the coition, which invades her individuality and introduces an alien element through penetration and internal fertilization. Although she may feel the sexual urge as a personal need, since she seeks out the male when in heat, yet the sexual adventure is immediately experienced by her as an interior event and not as an outward relation to the world and to others.

But the fundamental difference between male and female mammals lies in this: the sperm, through which the life of the male is transcended in another, at the same instant becomes a stranger to him and separates from his body; so that the male recovers his individuality intact at the moment when he transcends it. The egg, on the contrary, begins to separate from the female body when, fully matured, it emerges from the follicle and falls into the oviduct; but if fertilized by a gamete from outside, it becomes attached again through implantation in the uterus. First violated, the female is then alienated—she becomes, in part, another than herself. She carries the fetus inside her abdomen until it reaches a stage of development that varies according to the species—the guinea-pig is born almost adult, the kangaroo still almost an embryo. Tenanted by another, who battens upon her substance throughout the period of pregnancy, the female is at once herself and other than herself; and after the birth she feeds the newborn upon the milk of her breasts. Thus it is not too clear when the new individual is to be regarded as autonomous: at the moment of fertilization, of birth, or of weaning? It is noteworthy that the more clearly the female appears as a separate individual, the more imperiously the continuity of life asserts itself against her separateness. The fish and the bird, which expel the egg from the body before the embryo develops, are less enslaved to their offspring than is the female mammal. She regains some autonomy after the birth of her offspring—a certain distance is established between her and them; and it is following upon a separation that she devotes herself to them. She displays initiative and inventiveness in their behalf; she battles to defend them against other animals and may even become aggressive. But normally she does not seek to affirm her individuality; she is not hostile to males or to other females and shows little combative instinct.[1] In spite of Darwin's theory of sexual selection, now much disputed, she accepts without discrimination whatever male happens to be at hand. It is not that the female lacks individual abilities—quite the contrary. At times when she is free from maternal servitude she can now and then equal the male; the mare is as fleet as the stallion, the hunting bitch has as keen a nose as the dog, she-monkeys in tests show as much intelligence as males. It is only that this individuality is not laid claim to; the female renounces it for the benefit of the species, which demands this abdication.

The lot of the male is quite different. As we have just seen, even in his transcendence towards the next generation he keeps himself apart and maintains his individuality within himself. This characteristic is constant, from the insect to the highest animals. Even in the fishes and whales, which live peaceably in mixed schools, the males separate from the rest at the time of rut, isolate themselves, and become aggressive towards other males. Immediate, direct in the female, sexuality is indirect, it is experienced through inter-mediate circumstances, in the male. There is a distance between desire and satisfaction which he actively surmounts; he pushes, seeks out, touches the female, caresses and quiets her before he penetrates her. The organs used in such activities are, as I have remarked, often better developed in the male than in the female. It is notable that the living impulse that brings about the vast production of sperms is expressed also in the male by the appearance of bright plumage, brilliant scales, horns, antlers, a mane, by his voice, his exuberance. We no longer believe that the 'wedding finery' put on by the male during rut, nor his seductive posturings, have selective significance; but they do manifest the power of life, bursting forth in him with useless and

[1] Certain fowls wrangle over the best places in the poultry-yard and establish a hierarchy of dominance (the 'peck-order'); and sometimes among cattle there are cows that will fight for the leadership of the herd in the absence of males.

magnificent splendour. This vital superabundance, the activities directed towards mating, and the dominating affirmation of his power over the female in coitus itself—all this contributes to the assertion of the male individual as such at the moment of his living transcendence. In this respect Hegel is right in seeing the subjective element in the male, while the female remains wrapped up in the species. Subjectivity and separateness immediately signify conflict. Aggressiveness is one of the traits of the rutting male ; and it is not explained by competition for mates, since the number of females is about equal to the number of males ; it is rather the competition that is explained by this will to combat. It might be said that before procreating, the male claims as his own the act that perpetuates the species, and in doing battle with his peers confirms the truth of his individuality. The species takes residence in the female and absorbs most of her individual life ; the male on the contrary integrates the specific vital force into his individual life. No doubt he also submits to powers beyond his control: the sperms are formed within him and periodically he feels the rutting urge ; but these processes involve the sum total of the organism in much less degree than does the oestrus cycle. The production of sperms is not exhausting, nor is the actual production of eggs ; it is the development of the fertilized egg inside an adult animal that constitutes for the female an engrossing task. Coition is a rapid operation and one that robs the male of little vitality. He displays almost no paternal instinct. Very often he abandons the female after copulation. When he remains near her as head of a family group— monogamic family, harem, or herd—he nurtures and protects the community as a whole ; only rarely does he take a direct interest in the young. In the species capable of high individual development, the urge of the male towards autonomy—which in lower animals is his ruin—is crowned with success. He is in general larger than the female, stronger, swifter, more adventurous ; he leads a more independent life, his activities are more spontaneous ; he is more masterful, more imperious. In mammalian societies it is always he who commands.

In nature nothing is ever perfectly clear. The two types, male and female, are not always sharply distinguished ; while they sometimes exhibit a dimorphism—in coat colour or in arrangement of spotting or mottling—that seems absolutely distinctive, yet it may happen, on the contrary, that they are indistinguishable and that even their functions are hardly differentiated, as in many fishes. All in all, however, and especially at the top of the animal scale, the two sexes represent two diverse aspects of the life of the species. The difference between them is not, as has been claimed, that between activity and passivity; for the nucleus of the egg is active and moreover the development of the embryo is an active, living process, not a mechanical unfolding. It would be too simple to define the difference as that between change and permanence: for the sperm can create only because its vitality is maintained in the fertilized egg, and the egg can persist only through developmental change, without which it deteriorates and disappears.

It is true, however, that in these two processes, *maintaining* and *creating* (both of which are active), the synthesis of becoming is not accomplished in the same manner. To *maintain* is to deny the scattering of instants, it is to establish continuity in their flow; to *create* is to strike out from temporal unity in general an irreducible, separate present. And it is true also that in the female it is the continuity of life that seeks accomplishment in spite of separation; while separation into new and individualized forces is incited by male initiative. The male is thus permitted to express himself freely; the energy of the species is well integrated into his own living activity. On the contrary, the individuality of the female is opposed by the interest of the species; it is as if she were possessed by foreign forces—alienated. And this explains why the contrast between the sexes is not reduced when—as in higher forms—the individuality of the organisms concerned is more pronounced. On the contrary, the contrast is increased. The male finds more and more varied ways in which to employ the forces he is master of; the female feels her enslavement more and more keenly, the conflict between her own interests and the reproductive forces is heightened. Parturition in cows and mares is much more painful and dangerous than it is in mice and rabbits. Woman—the most individualized of females—seems to be the most fragile, most subject to this pain and danger: she who most dramatically fulfils the call of destiny and most profoundly differs from her male.

In man as in most animals the sexes are born in approximately equal numbers, the sex ratio for Western man being about 105.5 males to 100 females. Embryological development is analogous in the two sexes; however, in the female

47

embryo the primitive germinal epithelium (from which ovary or testis develops) remains neutral longer and is therefore under the hormonal influence for a longer time, with the result that its development may be more often reversed. Thus it may be that the majority of pseudo-hermaphrodites[1] are genotypically female subjects that have later become masculinized. One might suppose that the male organization is defined as such at the beginning, whereas the female embryo is slower in taking on its feminity; but these early phenomena of fetal life are still too little known to permit of any certainty in interpretation.

Once established, the genital systems correspond in the two sexes, and the sex hormones of both belong to the same chemical group, that of the sterols; all are derived in the last analysis from cholesterol. They regulate the secondary sexual differences of the soma. Neither the chemical formulae of the hormones nor the anatomical peculiarities are sufficient to define the human female as such. It is her functional development that distinguishes her especially from the male.

The development of the male is comparatively simple. From birth to puberty his growth is almost regular; at the age of fifteen or sixteen spermatogenesis begins, and it continues into old age; with its appearance hormones are produced that establish the masculine bodily traits. From this point on, the male sex life is normally integrated with his individual existence: in desire and in coition his transcendence towards the species is at one with his subjectivity —he *is* his body.

Woman's story is much more complex. In embryonic life the supply of oocytes is already built up, the ovary containing about 40,000 immature eggs, each in a follicle, of which perhaps 400 will ultimately reach maturation. From birth, the species has taken possession of woman and tends to tighten its grasp. In coming into the world woman experiences a kind of first puberty, as the oocytes enlarge suddenly; then the ovary is reduced to about a fifth of its former size—

[1] This difficult subject is magnificently treated from every point of view in H. H. YOUNG'S *Genital Abnormalities, Hermaphroditism, and Related Adrenal Diseases* (Baltimore, 1937). According to Dr. Young, only twenty cases of true hermaphroditism in man have been medically attested; but pseudo-hermaphrodites —having gonads of one sex with genitalia and sometimes secondary sex characters of the opposite sex—are numerous.— TR.

one might say that the child is granted a respite. While her body develops, her genital system remains almost stationary; some of the follicles enlarge, but they fail to mature. The growth of the little girl is similar to that of the boy; at the same age she is sometimes even taller and heavier than he is. But at puberty the species reasserts its claim. Under the influence of the ovarian secretions the number of developing follicles increases, the ovary receives more blood and grows larger, one of the follicles matures, ovulation occurs, and the menstrual cycle is initiated; the genital system assumes its definitive size and form, the body takes on feminine contours, and the endocrine balance is established.

It is to be noted that this whole occurrence has the aspect of a *crisis*. Not without resistance does the body of woman permit the species to take over; and this struggle is weakening and dangerous. Before puberty almost as many boys die as girls; from age fourteen to eighteen, 128 girls die to 100 boys, and from eighteen to twenty-two, 105 girls to 100 boys.[1] At this period frequently appear such diseases as chlorosis, tuberculosis, scoliosis (curvature of the spine), and osteomyelitis (inflammation of the bone marrow). In some cases puberty is abnormally precocious, appearing as early as age four or five. In others, on the contrary, puberty fails to become established, the subject remaining infantile and suffering from disorders of menstruation (amenorrhea or dysmenorrhea). Certain women shows signs of virilism, taking on masculine traits as a result of excessive adrenal secretion.

Such abnormalities in no way represent victories of the individual over the species; there is no way of escape, for as it enslaves the individual life, the species simultaneously supports and nourishes it. This duality is expressed at the level of the ovarian functions, since the vitality of woman has its roots in the ovaries as that of man in the testicles. In both sexes a castrated individual is not merely sterile; he or she suffers regression, degenerates. Not properly constituted, the whole organism is impoverished and thrown out of balance; it can expand and flourish only as its genital system

[1] Recent statistics show that in the United States among the white population there is no age level at which the death rate for women is higher than that of men. Among Negroes where conditions are doubtless less favourable on the average, the female death rate is higher only between the ages of fifteen and nineteen. (SCHEINFELD, *Women and Men*, chap. XVI, Harcourt, Brace & Co., 1943.)—TR.

49

expands and flourishes. And furthermore many reproductive phenomena are unconcerned with the individual life of the subject and may even be sources of danger. The mammary glands, developing at puberty, play no role in woman's individual economy: they can be excised at any time of life. Many of the ovarian secretions function for the benefit of the egg, promoting its maturation and adapting the uterus to its requirements; in respect to the organism as a whole they make for disequilibration rather than for regulation—the woman is adapted to the needs of the egg rather than to her own requirements.

From puberty to menopause woman is the theatre of a play that unfolds within her and in which she is not personally concerned. Anglo-Saxons call menstruation 'the curse'; in truth the menstrual cycle is a burden, and a useless one from the point of view of the individual. In Aristotle's time it was believed that each month blood flowed away that was intended, if fertilization had occurred, to build up the blood and flesh of the infant, and the truth of that old notion lies in the fact that over and over again woman does sketch in outline the groundwork of gestation. In lower mammals this oestrus cycle is confined to a particular season, and it is not accompanied by a flow of blood; only in the primates (monkeys, apes, and the human species) is it marked each month by blood and more or less pain.[1] During about fourteen days one of the Graafian follicles that enclose the eggs enlarges and matures, secreting the hormone folliculin (estrin). Ovulation occurs on about the fourteenth day: the follicle protrudes through the surface of the ovary and breaks open (sometimes with slight bleeding), the egg passes into the oviduct, and the wound develops into the corpus luteum. The latter secretes the hormone progesterone, which acts on the uterus during the second phase of the cycle. The lining of the uterus becomes thickened and glandular and full of blood vessels, forming in the womb a cradle to receive the fertilized egg. These cellular prolifera-

[1] 'Analysis of these phenomena in recent years has shown that they are similar in woman and the higher monkeys and apes, especially in the genus Rhesus. *It is evidently easier to experiment with these animals,*' writes Louis Gallien (*La Sexualité*).

[In the United States extensive research has been done on the sex physiology of the larger apes by Yerkes and others, especially at the Laboratories of Primate Biology at Yale University and in Florida (ROBERT M. YERKES, *Champanzees*, Yale University Press, 1943).—TR.]

tions being irreversible, the edifice is not resorbed if fertilization has not occurred. In the lower mammals the debris may escape gradually or may be carried away by the lymphatic vessels ; but in woman and the other primates, the thickened lining membrane (endometrium) breaks down suddenly, the blood vessels and blood spaces are opened, and the bloody mass trickles out as the menstrual flow. Then, while the corpus luteum regresses, the membrane that lines the uterus is reconstituted and a new follicular phase of the cycle begins.

This complex process, still mysterious in many of its details, involves the whole female organism, since there are hormonal reactions between the ovaries and other endocrine organs, such as the pituitary, the thyroid, and the adrenals, which affect the central nervous system, the sympathetic nervous system, and in consequence all the viscera. Almost all women—more than 85 per cent—show more or less distressing symptoms during the menstrual period. Blood pressure rises before the beginning of the flow and falls afterwards ; the pulse rate and often the temperature are increased, so that fever is frequent ; pains in the abdomen are felt ; often a tendency to constipation followed by diarrhoea is observed ; frequently there are also swelling of the liver, retention of urea, and albuminuria ; many subjects have sore throat and difficulties with hearing and sight ; perspiration is increased and accompanied at the beginning of the menses by an odour *sui generis,* which may be very strong and may persist throughout the period. The rate of basal metabolism is raised. The red blood count drops. The blood carries substances usually put on reserve in the tissues, especially calcium salts ; the presence of these substances reacts on the ovaries, on the thyroid—which enlarges—and on the pituitary (regulator of the changes in the uterine lining described above)—which becomes more active. This glandular instability brings on a pronounced nervous instability. The central nervous system is affected, with frequent headache, and the sympathetic system is overactive ; unconscious control through the central system is reduced, freeing convulsive reflexes and complexes and leading to a marked capriciousness of disposition. The woman is more emotional, more nervous, more irritable than usual, and may manifest serious psychic disturbance. It is during her periods that she feels her body most painfully as an obscure, alien thing ; it is, indeed, the prey of a stubborn and foreign life that each month constructs and then tears down a cradle within it ;

each month all things are made ready for a child and then aborted in the crimson flow. Woman, like man, *is* her body ;[1] but her body is something other than herself.

Woman experiences a more profound alienation when fertilization has occurred and the dividing egg passes down into the uterus and proceeds to develop there. True enough, pregnancy is a normal process, which, if it takes place under normal conditions of health and nutrition, is not harmful to the mother ; certain interactions between her and the fetus become established which are even beneficial to her. In spite of an optimistic view having all too obvious social utility, however, gestation is a fatiguing task of no individual benefit to the woman[2] but on the contrary demanding heavy sacrifices. It is often associated in the first months with loss of appetite and vomiting, which are not observed in any female domesticated animal and which signalize the revolt of the organism against the invading species.[3] There is a loss of phosphorus, calcium, and iron—the last difficult to make good later ; metabolic overactivity excites the endocrine system ; the sympathetic nervous system is in a state of increased excitement ; and the blood shows a lowered specific gravity, it is lacking in iron, and in general it is similar 'to that of persons fasting, of victims of famine, of those who have been bled frequently, of convalescents'.[4] All that a healthy and well-nourished woman can hope for is to recoup these losses without too much difficulty after childbirth ; but frequently serious accidents or at least dangerous disorders mark the course of pregnancy ; and if the woman is not strong, if hygienic precautions are not taken, repeated childbearing will make her prematurely old and misshapen, as often among the rural poor. Childbirth itself is painful and dangerous. In this crisis it is most clearly evident that the body does not always work to the advantage of both species and individual at once ; the infant may die, and again, in being born it may kill its mother or leave her with a chronic

[1] 'So I am my body, in so far, at least, as my experience goes, and conversely my body is like a life-model, or like a preliminary sketch, for my total being.' (MERLEAU-PONTY, *Phénoménologie de la perception.*)
[2] I am taking here an exclusively physiological point of view. It is evident that maternity can be very advantageous psychologically for a woman, just as it can also be a disaster.
[3] It may be said that these symptoms also signalize a faulty diet, according to some modern gynaecologists.—TR.
[4] Cf. H. VIGNES in the *Traité de physiologie,* vol. XI, edited by Roger and Binet.

ailment. Nursing is also a tiring service. A number of factors —especially the hormone prolactin—bring about the secretion of milk in the mammary glands; some soreness and often fever may accompany the process and in any case the nursing mother feeds the newborn from the resources of her own vitality. The conflict between species and individual, which sometimes assumes dramatic force at childbirth, endows the feminine body with a disturbing frailty. It has been well said that women 'have infirmity in the abdomen'; and it is true that they have within them a hostile element—it is the species gnawing at their vitals. Their maladies are often caused not by some infection from without but by some internal maladjustment; for example, a false inflammation of the endometrium is set up through the reaction of the uterine lining to an abnormal excitation of the ovaries; if the corpus luteum persists instead of declining after menstruation, it causes inflammation of the oviducts and uterine lining, and so on.

In the end woman escapes the iron grasp of the species by way of still another serious crisis; the phenomena of the menopause, the inverse of puberty, appear between the ages of forty-five and fifty. Ovarian activity diminishes and disappears, with resulting impoverishment of the individual's vital forces. It may be supposed that the metabolic glands, the thyroid and pituitary, are compelled to make up in some fashion for the functioning of the ovaries; and thus, along with the depression natural to the change of life, are to be noted signs of excitation, such as high blood pressure, hot flushes, nervousness, and sometimes increased sexuality. Some women develop fat deposits at this time; others become masculinized. In many, a new endocrine balance becomes established. Woman is now delivered from the servitude imposed by her female nature; but she is not to be likened to a eunuch, for her vitality is unimpaired. And what is more, she is no longer the prey of overwhelming forces; she is herself, she and her body are one. It is sometimes said that women of a certain age constitute 'a third sex'; and, in truth, while they are not males, they are no longer females. Often, indeed, this release from female physiology is expressed in a health, a balance, a vigour that they lacked before.

In addition to the primary sexual characteristics, woman has various secondary sexual peculiarities that are more or less directly produced in consequence of the first, through hormonal action. On the average she is shorter than the male and lighter, her skeleton is more delicate, and the pelvis is larger in adaptation to the functions of pregnancy and childbirth ; her connective tissues accumulate fat and her contours are thus more rounded than those of the male. Appearance in general—structure, skin, hair—is distinctly different in the two sexes. Muscular strength is much less in woman, about two thirds that of man ; she has less respiratory capacity, the lungs and trachea being smaller. The larynx is relatively smaller, and in consequence the female voice is higher. The specific gravity of the blood is lower in woman and there is less haemoglobin ; women are therefore less robust and more disposed to anaemia than are males. Their pulse is more rapid, the vascular system less stable, with ready blushing. Instability is strikingly characteristic of woman's organization in general ; among other things, man shows greater stability in the metabolism of calcium, woman fixing much less of this material and losing a good deal during menstruation and pregnancy. It would seem that in regard to calcium the ovaries exert a catabolic action, with resulting instability that brings on difficulties in the ovaries and in the thyroid, which is more developed in woman than in man. Irregularities in the endocrine secretions react on the sympathetic nervous system, and nervous and muscular control is uncertain. This lack in stability and control underlies woman's emotionalism, which is bound up with circulatory fluctuations—palpitation of the heart, blushing, and so forth—and on this account women are subject to such displays of agitation as tears, hysterical laughter, and nervous crises.

It is obvious once more than many of these traits originate in woman's subordination to the species, and here we find the most striking conclusion of this survey ; namely, that woman is of all mammalian females at once the one who is most profoundly alienated (her individuality the prey of outside forces), and the one who most violently resists this alienation ; in no other is enslavement of the organism to reproduction more imperious or more unwillingly accepted. Crises of puberty and the menopause, monthly 'curse', long and often difficult pregnancy, painful and sometimes dangerous childbirth, illnesses, unexpected symptoms and complications—these are characteristic of the human female. It would seem that her lot is heavier than that of other females in just about the same degree that she goes beyond other females in the assertion of her individuality. In comparison with her the male seems infinitely favoured: his sexual life is not in opposition to his existence as a person, and biologically it runs an even course, without crises and generally without mishap. On the average, women live as long as men, or longer; but they are much more often ailing, and there are many times when they are not in command of themselves.

These biological considerations are extremely important. In the history of woman they play a part of the first rank and constitute an essential element in her situation. Throughout our further discussion we shall always bear them in mind. For, the body being the instrument of our grasp upon the world, the world is bound to seem a very different thing when apprehended in one manner or another. This accounts for our lengthy study of the biological facts; they are one of the keys to the understanding of woman. But I deny that they establish for her a fixed and inevitable destiny. They are insufficient for setting up a hierarchy of the sexes; they fail to explain why woman is the Other; they do not condemn her to remain in this subordinate role for ever.

It has frequently been maintained that in physiology alone must be sought the answers to these questions: Are the chances for individual success the same in the two sexes? Which plays the more important role in the species? But it must be noted that the first of these problems is quite different in the case of woman, as compared with other females; for animal species are fixed and it is possible to define them in static terms—by merely collecting observations it can be decided whether the mare is as fast as the stallion, or whether male chimpanzees excel their mates in intelligence tests—whereas the human species is for ever in a state of change, for ever becoming.

Certain materialistic savants have approached the problem in a purely static fashion; influenced by the theory of psychophysiological parallelism, they sought to work out mathematical comparisons between the male and female organism—and they imagined that these measurements registered directly the functional capacities of the two sexes. For example, these students have been engaged in elaborately trifling discussions regarding the absolute and relative weight of the brain in man and woman—with inconclusive results, after all corrections have been made. But what destroys much of the interest of these careful researches is the fact that it has not been possible to establish any relation whatever between the weight of the brain and the level of intelligence. And one would similarly be at loss to present a psychic interpretation of the chemical formulae designating the male and female hormones.

As for the present study, I categorically reject the notion of psychophysiological parallelism, for it is a doctrine whose foundations have long since been thoroughly undermined. If I mention it at all, it is because it still haunts many minds in spite of its philosophical and scientific bankruptcy. I reject also any comparative system that assumes the existence of a *natural* hierarchy or scale of values—for example, an evolutionary hierarchy. It is vain to ask if the female body is or is not more infantile than that of the male, if it is more or less similar to that of the apes, and so on. All these dissertations which mingle a vague naturalism with a still more vague ethics or aesthetics are pure verbiage. It is only in a human perspective that we can compare the female and the male of the human species. But man is defined as a being who is not fixed, who makes himself what he is. As Merleau-Ponty very justly puts it, man is not a natural species: he is a historical idea. Woman is not a completed reality, but rather a becoming, and it is in her becoming that she should be compared with man ; that is to say, her *possibilities* should be defined. What gives rise to much of the debate is the tendency to reduce her to what she has been, to what she is today, in raising the question of her capabilities ; for the fact is that capabilities are clearly manifested only when they have been realized— but the fact is also that when we have to do with a being whose nature is transcendent action, we can never close the books.

Nevertheless it will be said that if the body is not a *thing*, it is a situation, as viewed in the perspective I am adopting— that of Heidegger, Sartre, and Merleau-Ponty: it is the instrument of our grasp upon the world, a limiting factor for our projects. Woman is weaker than man, she has less muscular strength, fewer red blood corpuscles, less lung capacity, she runs more slowly, can lift less heavy weights, can compete with man in hardly any sport ; she cannot stand up to him in a fight. To all this weakness must be added the instability, the lack of control, and the fragility already discussed : these are facts. Her grasp on the world is thus more restricted ; she has less firmness and less steadiness available for projects that in general she is less capable of carrying out. In other words, her individual life is less rich than man's.

Certainly these facts cannot be denied—but in themselves they have no significance. Once we adopt the human perspective, interpreting the body on a basis of existence, biology becomes an abstract science; whenever the physiological fact (for instance, muscular inferiority) takes on meaning, this meaning is at once seen as dependent on a whole context; the 'weakness' is revealed as such only in the light of the ends man proposes, the instruments he has available, and the laws he establishes. If he does not wish to seize the world, then the idea of a *grasp* on things has no sense; when in this seizure the full employment of bodily power is not required, above the available minimum, then differences in strength are annulled; wherever violence is contrary to custom, muscular force cannot be a basis for domination. In brief, the concept of *weakness* can be defined only with reference to existentialist, economic, and moral considerations. It has been said that the human species is anti-natural, a statement that is hardly exact, since man cannot deny facts; but he establishes their truth by the way in which he deals with them; nature has reality for him only to the extent that it is involved in his activity—his own nature not excepted. As with her grasp on the world, it is again impossible to measure in the abstract the burden imposed on woman by her reproductive function. The bearing of maternity upon the individual life, regulated naturally in animals by the oestrus cycle and the seasons, is not definitely prescribed in woman—society alone is the arbiter. The bondage of woman to the species is more or less rigorous according to the number of births demanded by society and the degree of hygienic care provided for pregnancy and childbirth. Thus, while it is true that in the higher animals the individual existence is asserted more imperiously by the male than by the female, in the human species individual 'possibilities' depend upon the economic and social situation.

But in any case it does not always happen that the male's individual privileges give him a position of superiority within the species, for in maternity the female acquires a kind of autonomy of her own. Sometimes, as in the baboons studied by Zuckermann,[1] the male does dominate; but in many species the two members of the pair lead a separate

[1] *The Social Life of Monkeys and Apes* (1932).

life, and in the lion the two sexes share equally in the duties of the den. Here again the human situation cannot be reduced to any other; it is not as single individuals that human beings are to be defined in the first place; men and women have never stood opposed to each other in single combat; the couple is an original *Mitsein*, a basic combination; and as such it always appears as a permanent or temporary element in a larger collectivity.

Within such a society, which is more necessary to the species, male or female? At the level of the gametes, at the level of the biological functions of coition and pregnancy, the male principle creates to maintain, the female principle maintains to create, as we have seen; but what are the various aspects of this division of labour in different forms of social life? In sessile species, attached to other organisms or to substrata, in those furnished by nature with abundant sustenance obtainable without effort, the role of the male is limited to fecundation; where it is necessary to seek, to hunt, to fight in order to provide the food needed by the young, the male in many cases co-operates in their support. This co-operation becomes absolutely indispensable in a species where the offspring remain unable to take care of themselves for a long time after weaning; here the male's assistance becomes extremely important, for the lives he has begotten cannot be maintained without him. A single male can fecundate a number of females each year; but it requires a male for every female to assure the survival of the offspring after they are born, to defend them against enemies, to wrest from nature the wherewithal to satisfy their needs. In human history the equilibrium between the forces of production and of reproduction is brought about by different means under different economic conditions, and these conditions govern the relations of male and female to offspring and in consequence to each other. But here we are leaving the realm of biology; by its light alone we could never decide the primacy of one sex or the other in regard to the perpetuation of the species.

But in truth a society is not a species, for it is in a society that the species attains the status of existence—transcending itself towards the world and towards the future. Its ways and customs cannot be deduced from biology, for the individuals that compose the society are never abandoned to the dictates of their nature; they are subject rather to that second nature which is custom and in which are reflected the desires and the fears that express their essential nature. It is not merely as a body, but rather as a body subject to taboos, to laws, that the subject is conscious of himself and attains fulfilment—it is with reference to certain values that he evaluates himself. And, once again, it is not upon physiology that values can be based; rather, the facts of biology take on the values that the existent bestows upon them. If the respect or the fear inspired by woman prevents the use of violence towards her, then the muscular superiority of the male is no source of power. If custom decrees—as in certain Indian tribes—that the young girls are to choose their husbands, or if the father dictates the marriage choice, then the sexual aggressiveness of the male gives him no power of initiative, no advantage. The close bond between mother and child will be for her a source of dignity according to the value placed upon the child—which is highly variable—and this very bond, as we have seen, will be recognized or not according to the presumptions of the society concerned.

Thus we must view the facts of biology in the light of an ontological, economic, social, and psychological context. The enslavement of the female to the species and the limitations of her various powers are extremely important facts; the body of woman is one of the essential elements in her situation in the world. But that body is not enough to define her as woman; there is no true living reality except as manifested by the conscious individual through activities and in the bosom of a society. Biology is not enough to give an answer to the question that is before us: why is woman the *Other*? Our task is to discover how the nature of woman has been affected throughout the course of history; we are concerned to find out what humanity has made of the human female.

CHAPTER II

THE PSYCHOANALYTIC POINT OF VIEW

T H E tremendous advance accomplished by psychoanalysis over psychophysiology lies in the view that no
factor becomes involved in the psychic life without
having taken on human significance ; it is not the body-object
described by biologists that actually exists, but the body as
lived in by the subject. Woman is a female to the extent that
she feels herself as such. There are biologically essential
features that are not a part of her real, experienced situation :
thus the structure of the egg is not reflected in it, but on
the contrary an organ of no great biological importance,
like the clitoris, plays in it a part of the first rank. It is not
nature that defines woman ; it is she who defines herself
by dealing with nature on her own account in her emotional
life.

An entire system has been built up in this perspective,
which I do not intend to criticize as a whole, merely examining its contribution to the study of woman. It is not an easy
matter to discuss psychoanalysis *per se*. Like all religions—
Christianity and Marxism, for example—it displays an embarrassing flexibility on a basis of rigid concepts. Words are
sometimes used in their most literal sense, the term *phallus*,
for example, designating quite exactly that fleshy projection
which marks the male ; again, they are indefinitely expanded
and take on symbolic meaning, the phallus now expressing
the virile character and situation *in toto*. If you attack the
letter of his doctrine, the psychoanalyst protests that you
misunderstand its spirit ; if you applaud its spirit, he at once
wishes to confine you to the letter. The doctrine is of no importance, says one, psychoanalysis is a method ; but the success of the method strengthens the doctrinaire in his faith.
After all, where is one to find the true lineaments of psychoanalysis if not among the psychoanalysts? But there are here-
tics among these, just as there are among Christians and
Marxists ; and more than one psychoanalyst has declared that
'the worst enemies of psychoanalysis are the pyschoanalysts.'

In spite of a scholastic precision that often becomes pedantic, many obscurities remain to be dissipated. As Sartre and Merleau-Ponty have observed, the proposition 'Sexuality is co-extensive with existence' can be understood in two very different ways; it can mean that every appearance of the existent has a sexual significance, or that every sexual phenomenon has an existential import. It is possible to reconcile these statements, but too often one merely slips from one to the other. Furthermore, as soon as the 'sexual' is distinguished from the 'genital', the idea of sexuality becomes none too clear. According to Dalbiez, 'the sexual with Freud is the intrinsic aptitude for releasing the genital'. But nothing is more obscure than the idea of 'aptitude'—that is, of possibility—for only realization gives indubitable proof of what is possible. Not being a philosopher, Freud has justly refused to justify his system philosophically; and his disciples maintain that on this account he is exempt from all metaphysical attack. There are metaphysical assumptions behind all his dicta, however, and to use his language is to adopt a philosophy. It is just such confusions that call for criticism, while making criticism difficult.

Freud never showed much concern with the destiny of woman; it is clear that he simply adapted his account from that of the destiny of man, with slight modifications. Earlier the sexologist Marañon had stated that 'As specific energy, we may say that the libido is a force of virile character. We will say as much of the orgasm.' According to him, women who attain orgasm are 'viriloid' women; the sexual impulse is 'in one direction' and the woman is only half way along the road. Freud never goes to such an extreme; he admits that woman's sexuality is evolved as fully as man's; but he hardly studies it in particular. He writes: 'The libido is constantly and regularly male in essence, whether it appears in man or in woman.' He declines to regard the feminine libido as having its own original nature, and therefore it will necessarily seem to him like a complex deviation from the human libido in general. This develops at first, he thinks, identically in the two sexes—each infant passes first through an oral phase that fixates it upon the maternal breast, and then through an anal phase; finally it reached the genital phase, at which point the sexes become differentiated.

Freud further brought to light a fact the importance of which had not been fully appreciated: namely, that masculine erotism is definitely located in the penis, whereas in woman
61

there are two distinct erotic systems: one the clitoral, which develops in childhood, the other vaginal, which develops only after puberty. When the boy reaches the genital phase, his evolution is completed, though he must pass from the auto-erotic inclination, in which pleasure is subjective, to the hetero-erotic inclination, in which pleasure is bound up with an object, normally woman. This transition is made at the time of puberty through a narcissistic phase. But the penis will remain, as in childhood, the specific organ of erotism. Woman's libido, also passing through a narcissistic phase, will become objective, normally towards man; but the process will be much more complex, because woman must pass from clitoral pleasure to vaginal. There is only one genital stage for man, but there are two for woman; she runs a much greater risk of not reaching the end of her sexual evolution, of remaining at the infantile stage and thus of developing neuroses.

While still in the auto-erotic stage, the child becomes more or less strongly attached to an object. The boy becomes fixed on his mother and desires to identify himself with his father; this presumption terrifies him and he dreads mutilation at the hands of his father in punishment for it. Thus the castration complex springs from the Oedipus complex. Then aggressiveness towards the father develops, but at the same time the child interiorizes the father's authority; thus the super-ego is built up in the child and censures his incestuous tendencies. These are repressed, the complex is liquidated, and the son is freed from his fear of his father, whom he has now installed in his own psyche under the guise of moral precepts.[1] The super-ego is more powerful in proportion as the Oedipus complex has been more marked and more rigorously resisted.

Freud at first described the little girl's history in a completely corresponding fashion, later calling the feminine form of the process the Electra complex; but it is clear that he defined it less in itself than upon the basis of his masculine pattern. He recognized a very important difference between the two, however: the little girl at first has a mother fixation, but the boy is at no time sexually attracted to the father. This fixation of the girl represents a survival of the oral phase. Then the child identifies herself with the father; but towards

[1] 'The super-ego or conscience is a precipitate of all the prohibitions and inhibitions that were originally inculcated into us by our parents, especially by the father.' (BRILL, *Freud's Contribution to Psychiatry* [W. W. Norton & Co., 1944], p. 153).—TR.

the age of five she dicovers the anatomical difference between
the sexes, and she reacts to the absence of the penis by
acquiring a castration complex—she imagines that she has
been mutilated and is pained at the thought. Having then to
renounce her virile pretensions, she identifies herself with her
mother and seeks to seduce the father. The castration complex and the Electra complex thus reinforce each other. Her
feeling of frustration is the keener since, loving her father,
she wished in vain to be like him ; and, inversely, her regret
strengthens her love, for she is able to compensate for her inferiority through the affection she inspires in her father. The
little girl entertains a feeling of rivalry and hostility towards
her mother. Then the super-ego is built up also in her, and the
incestuous tendencies are repressed ; but her super-ego is not
so strong, for the Electra complex is less sharply defined than
the Oedipus because the first fixation was upon the mother,
and since the father is himself the object of the love that he
condemns, his prohibitions are weaker than in the case of
his son-rival. It can be seen that like her genital development the whole sexual drama is more complex for the girl
than for her brothers. In consequence she may be led to react to the castration complex by denying her femininity, by
continuing obstinately to covet a penis and to identify herself with her father. This attitude will cause her to remain
in the clitoral phase, to become frigid, or turn towards homo-
sexuality.

The two essential objections that may be raised against
this view derive from the fact that Freud based it upon a
masculine model. He assumes that woman feels that she is a
mutilated man. But the idea of mutilation implies comparison
and evaluation. Many psychoanalysts today admit that the
young girl may regret not having a penis without believing,
however, that it has been removed from her body ; and even
this regret is not general. It could not arise from a simple
anatomical comparison ; many little girls, in fact, are late
in discovering the masculine construction, and if they do, it is
only by sight. The little boy obtains from his penis a living
experience that makes it an object of pride to him, but this
pride does not necessarily imply a corresponding humiliation
for his sisters, since they know the masculine organ in its outward aspect only—this outgrowth, this weak little rod of flesh
can in itself inspire them only with indifference, or even disgust. The little girl's covetousness, when it exists, results from
a previous evaluation of virility. Freud takes this for granted,

when it should be accounted for.[1] On the other hand, the concept of the Electra complex is very vague, because it is not supported by a basic description of the feminine libido. Even in boys the occurrence of a definitely genital Oedipus complex is by no means general ; but, apart from very few exceptions, it cannot be admitted that the father is a source of genital excitation for his young daughter. One of the great problems of feminine eroticism is that clitoral pleasure is localized ; and it is only towards puberty that a number of erogenous zones develop in various parts of the body, along with the growth of vaginal sensation. To say, then, that in a child of ten the kisses and caresses of her father have an 'intrinsic aptitude' for arousing clitoral pleasure is to assert something that in most cases is nonsense. If it is admitted that the Electra complex has only a very diffuse emotional character, then the whole question of emotion is raised. Freudianism does not help us in defining emotion as distinguished from sexuality. What deifies the father is by no means the feminine libido (nor is the mother deified by the desire she arouses in the son) ; on the contrary, the fact that the feminine desire (in the daughter) is directed towards a sovereign being gives it a special character. It does not determine the nature of its object ; rather it is affected by the latter. The sovereignty of the father is a fact of social origin, which Freud fails to account for ; in fact, he states that it is impossible to say what authority decided, at a certain moment in history, that the father should take precedence over the mother—a decision that, according to Freud, was progressive, but due to causes unknown. 'It could not have been patriarchal authority, since it is just this authority which progress conferred upon the father', as he puts it in his last work.[2]

Adler took issue with Freud because he saw the deficiency of a system that undertook to explain human life upon the basis of sexuality alone ; he holds that sexuality should be integrated with the total personality. With Freud all human behaviour seems to be the outcome of desire—that is, of the search for pleasure—but for Adler man appears to be aiming at certain goals ; for the sexual urge he substitutes motives, purposes, projects. He gives so large a place to the intelligence

[1] This discussion will be resumed at much greater length in Book Two (published as a separate volume, *The Second Sex*), chap. I.
[2] FREUD, *Moses and Monotheism*, translated by Katherine Jones (Alfred A. Knopf, 1939).

that often the sexual has in his eyes only a symbolic value. According to his system, the human drama can be reduced to three elemental factors: in every individual there is a *will to power*, which, however, is accompanied by an *inferiority complex*; the resulting conflict leads the individual to employ a thousand ruses in a *flight from reality*—a reality with which he fears he may not be able to cope; the subject thus withdraws to some degree from the society of which he is apprehensive and hence becomes afflicted with the neuroses that involve disturbance of the social attitude. In woman the inferiority complex takes the form of a shamed rejection of her femininity. It is not the lack of the penis that causes this complex, but rather woman's total situation; if the little girl feels penis envy it is only as the symbol of privileges enjoyed by boys. The place the father holds in the family, the universal predominance of males, her own education—everything confirms her in her belief in masculine superiority. Later on, when she takes part in sexual relations, she finds a new humiliation in the coital posture that places woman underneath the man. She reacts through the 'masculine protest': either she endeavours to masculinize herself or she makes use of her feminine weapons to wage war upon the male. Through maternity she may be able to find an equivalent of the penis in her child. But this supposes that she begins by wholly accepting her role as woman and that she assumes her inferiority. She is divided against herself much more profoundly than is the male.

I shall not enlarge here upon the theoretical differences that separate Adler and Freud nor upon the possibilities of a reconciliation; but this may be said: neither the explanation based upon the sexual urge nor that based upon motive is sufficient, for every urge poses a motive, but the motive is apprehended only through the urge—a synthesis of Adlerianism and Freudianism would therefore seem possible of realization. In fact, Adler retains the idea of psychic causation as an integral part of his system when he introduces the concepts of goal and of finality, and he is somewhat in accord with Freud in regard to the relation between drives and mechanism: the physicist always recognizes determinism when he is concerned with conflict or a force of attention. The axiomatic proposition held in common by all psychoanalysts is this: the human story is to be explained by the interplay of determinate elements. And all the psychoanalysts allot the same destiny to woman. Her drama is epitomized in the con-

C

flict between her 'viriloid' and her 'feminine' tendencies, the first expressed through the clitoral system, the second in vaginal erotism. As a child she identifies herself with her father ; then she becomes possessed with a feeling of inferiority with reference to the male and is faced with a dilemma : either to assert her independence and become virilized—which, with the underlying complex of inferiority, induces a state of tension that threatens neurosis—or to find happy fulfilment in amorous submission, a solution that is facilitated by her love for the sovereign father. He it is whom she really seeks in lover or husband, and thus her sexual love is mingled with the desire to be dominated. She will find her recompense in maternity, since that will afford her a new kind of independence. This drama would seem to be endowed with an energy, a dynamism, of its own ; it steadily pursues its course through any and all distorting incidents, and every woman is passively swept along in it.

The psychoanalysts have had no trouble in finding empirical confirmation for their theories. As we know, it was possible for a long time to explain the position of the planets on the Ptolemaic system by adding to it sufficiently subtle complications ; and by superposing an inverse Oedipus complex upon the Oedipus complex, by disclosing desire in all anxiety, success has been achieved in integrating with the Freudian system the very facts that appear to contradict its validity. It is possible to make out a form only against a background, and the way in which the form is apprehended brings out the background behind it in positive detail ; thus, if one is determined to describe a special case in a Freudian perspective, one will encounter the Freudian scheme behind it. But when a doctrine demands the indefinite and arbitrary multiplication of secondary explanations, when observation brings to light as many exceptions as instances conformable to rule, it is better to give up the old rigid framework. Indeed, every psychoanalyst today is busily engaged after his own fashion in making the Freudian concepts less rigid and in attempting compromise. For example, a contemporary psychoanalyst[1] writes as follows: "Wherever there is a complex, there are by definition a number of components . . . The complex consists in the association of these disparate elements and not in the representation of one among them by the others.' But the concept of a simple association of elements is unacceptable, for the psychic life is not a mosaic, it is a single whole in every one of its aspects

[1] BAUDOUIN, *L'Ame enfantine et la psychanalyse.*

and we must respect that unity. This is possible only by our recovering through the disparate facts the original purposiveness of existence. If we do not go back to this source, man appears to be the battleground of compulsions and prohibitions that alike are devoid of meaning and incidental.

All psychoanalysts systematically reject the idea of *choice* and the correlated concept of value, and therein lies the intrinsic weakness of the system. Having dissociated compulsions and prohibitions from the free choice of the existent, Freud fails to give us an explanation of their origin—he takes them for granted. He endeavoured to replace the idea of value with that of authority; but he admits in *Moses and Monotheism* that he has no way of accounting for this authority. Incest, for example, is forbidden because the father has forbidden it—but why did he forbid it? It is a mystery. The super-ego interiorizes, introjects commands and prohibitions emanating from an arbitrary tyranny, and the instinctive drives are there, we know not why: these two realities are unrelated because morality is envisaged as foreign to sexuality. The human unity appears to be disrupted, there is no thoroughfare from the individual to society; to reunite them Freud was forced to invent strange fictions, as in *Totem and Taboo*. Adler saw clearly that the castration complex could be explained only in social context; he grappled with the problem of valuation, but he did not reach the source in the individual values recognized by society, and he did not grasp the fact that values are involved in sexuality itself, which led him to misjudge its importance.

Sexuality most certainly plays a considerable role in human life; it can be said to pervade life throughout. We have already learned from physiology that the living activity of the testes and the ovaries is integrated with that of the body in general. The existent is a sexual, a sexuate body, and in his relations with other existents who are also sexuate bodies, sexuality is in consequence always involved. But if body and sexuality are concrete expressions of existence, it is with reference to this that their significance can be discovered. Lacking this perspective, psychoanalysis takes for granted unexplained facts. For instance, we are told that the little girl is *ashamed* of urinating in a squatting position with her bottom uncovered—but whence comes this shame? And likewise, before asking whether the male is proud of having a penis or whether his pride is expressed in his penis, it is necessary to know what pride is and how the aspirations of the subject can be incarnated in an object. There is no need of taking sexuality as an irreducible datum, for there is in the existent a more original 'quest of being', of which sexuality is only one of the aspects. Sartre demonstrates this truth in *L'Etre et le néant*, as does Bachelard in his works on Earth, Air, and Water. The psychoanalysts hold that the primary truth regarding man is his relation with his own body and with the bodies of his fellows in the group ;. but man has a primordial interest in the substance of the natural world which surrounds him and which he tries to discover in work, in play, and in all the experiences of the 'dynamic imagination'. Man aspires to be at one concretely with the whole world, apprehended in all possible ways. To work the earth, to dig a hole, are activities as original as the embrace, as coition, and they deceive themselves who see here no more than sexual symbols. The hole, the ooze, the gash, hardness, integrity are primary realities ; and the interest they have for man is not dictated by the libido, but rather the libido will be coloured by the manner in which he becomes aware of them. It is not because it symbolizes feminine virginity that integrity fascinates man ; but it is his admiration for integrity that renders virginity precious. Work, war, play, art signify ways of being concerned with the world which cannot be reduced to any others ; they disclose qualities that interfere with those which sexuality reveals. It is at once in their light and in the light of these erotic experiences that the individual exercises his power of choice. But only an ontological point of view, a comprehension of being in general, permits us to restore the unity of this choice.

It is this concept of choice, indeed, that psychoanalysis most vehemently rejects in the name of determinism and the 'collective unconscious' ; and it is this unconscious that is supposed to supply man with prefabricated imagery and a universal symbolism. Thus it would explain the observed analogies of dreams, of purposeless actions, of visions of delirium, of allegories, and of human destinies. To speak of liberty would be to deny oneself the possibility of explaining these disturbing conformities. But the idea of liberty is not incompatible with the existence of certain constants. If the psychoanalytic method is frequently rewarding in spite of the errors in its theory, that is because there are in every individual case certain factors of undeniable generality: situations and behaviour patterns constantly recur, and the moment of decision flashes from a cloud of generality and repetition. 'Anatomy is destiny', said Freud; and this phrase is echoed by that of Merleau-Ponty: 'The body is generality.' Existence is all one, bridging the gaps between individual existents; it makes itself manifest in analogous organisms, and therefore constant factors will be found in the bonds between the ontological and the sexual. At a given epoch of history the techniques, the economic and social structure of a society, will reveal to all its members an identical world, and there a constant relation of sexuality to social patterns will exist; analogous individuals, placed in analogous conditions, will see analogous points of significance in the given circumstances. This analogy does not establish a rigorous universality, but it accounts for the fact that general types may be recognized in individual case histories.

The symbol does not seem to me to be an allegory elaborated by a mysterious unconscious; it is rather the perception of a certain significance through the analogue of the significant object. Symbolic significance is manifested in the same way to numerous individuals, because of the identical situation connecting all the individual existents, and the identical set of artificial conditions that all must confront. Symbolism did not come down from heaven nor rise up from subterranean depths—it has been elaborated, like language, by that human reality which is at once *Mitsein* and separation; and this explains why individual invention also has its place, as in practice psychoanalysis has to admit, regardless of doctrine. Our perspective allows us, for example, to understand the value widely accorded to the penis.[1] It is impossible to account for it without taking our departure from an existential fact: the tendency of the subject towards *alienation*. The anxiety that his liberty induces in the subject leads him to search for himself in things, which is a kind of flight from himself. This tendency is so fundamental that immediately after weaning, when he is separated from the Whole, the infant is compelled to lay hold upon his alienated existence in mirrors and in the gaze of his parents. Primitive people are alienated in mana, in the totem; civilized people in their individual souls, in their egos, their names, their property, their work. Here is to be found the primary temptation to inauthenticity, to failure to be genuinely oneself. The penis is singulary adapted for playing this role of 'double' for the little boy—it is for him at once a foreign object and himself; it is a plaything, a doll,

[1] We shall return to this subject at greater length in Book Two, chap. I.

and yet his own flesh; relatives and nurse-girls behave towards it as if it were a little person. It is easy to see, then, how it becomes for the child 'an *alter ego* ordinarily more artful, more intelligent, and more clever than the individual'.[1] The penis is regarded by the subject as at once himself and other than himself, because the functions of urination and later of erection are processes midway between the voluntary and involuntary, and because it is a capricious and as it were a foreign source of pleasure that is felt subjectively. The individual's specific transcendence takes concrete form in the penis and it is a source of pride. Because the phallus is thus set apart, man can bring into integration with his subjective individuality the life that overflows from it. It is easy to see, then, that the length of the penis, the force of the urinary jet, the strength of erection and ejaculation become for him the measure of his own worth.[2]

Thus the incarnation of transcendence in the phallus is a constant; and since it is also a constant for the child to feel transcended—that is to say, frustrated in his own transcendence by the father—we therefore continually come upon the Freudian idea of the 'castration complex'. Not having that *alter ego*, the little girl is not alienated in a material thing and cannot retrieve her integrity. On this account she is led to make an object of her whole self, to set up herself as the Other. Whether she knows that she is or is not comparable with boys is secondary; the important point is that, even if she is unaware of it, the absence of the penis prevents her from being conscious of herself as a sexual being. From this flow many consequences. But the constants I have referred to do not for all that establish a fixed destiny—the phallus assumes such worth as it does because it symbolizes a dominance that is exercised in other domains. If woman should succeed in establishing herself as subject, she would invent equivalents of the phallus; in fact, the doll, incarnating the promise of the baby that is to come in the future, can

[1] ALICE BALINT, *La Vie intime de l'enfant*, p. 101.

[2] I have been told of peasant children amusing themselves in excremental competition; the one who produced the most copious and solid feces enjoyed a prestige unmatched by any other form of success, whether in games or even in fighting. The fecal mass here plays the same part as the penis—there is alienation in both cases.

[Pride in this peculiar type of eminence is by no means confined to European peasant children; it has been observed in young Americans and is doubtless well-nigh universal.—Tr.]

becomes a possession more precious than the penis.[1] There are matrilineal societies in which the women keep in their possession the *masks* in which the group finds alienation; in such societies the penis loses much of its glory. The fact is that a true human privilege is based upon the anatomical privilege only in virtue of the total situation. Psychoanalysis can establish its truths only in the historical context.

Woman can be defined by her consciousness of her own femininity no more satisfactorily than by saying that she is a female, for she acquires this consciousness under circumstances dependent upon the society of which she is a member. Interiorizing the unconscious and the whole psychic life, the very language of psychoanalysis suggests that the drama of the individual unfolds within him—such words as *complex*, *tendency*, and so on make that implication. But a life is a relation to the world, and the individual defines himself by making his own choices through the world about him. We must therefore turn towards the world to find answers for the questions we are concerned with. In particular psychoanalysis fails to explain why woman is the *Other*. For Freud himself admits that the prestige of the penis is explained by the sovereignty of the father, and, as we have seen, he confesses that he is ignorant regarding the origin of male supremacy.

We therefore decline to accept the method of psychoanalysis, without rejecting *en bloc* the contributions of the science or denying the fertility of some of its insights. In the first place, we do not limit ourselves to regarding sexuality as something given. The insufficiency of this view is shown by the poverty of the resulting descriptions of the feminine libido; as I have already said, the psychoanalysts have never studied it directly, but only in taking the male libido as their point of departure. They seem to ignore the fundamental ambivalence of the attraction exerted on the female by the male. Freudians and Adlerians explain the anxiety felt by the female confronted by the masculine sex as being the inversion of a frustrated desire. Stekel saw more clearly that an original reaction was concerned, but he accounts for it in a superficial manner. Woman, he says, would fear defloration, penetration, pregnancy, and pain, and such fear would restrain her desire —but this explanation is too rational. Instead of holding that

[1] We shall return to these ideas in the second part; I note them here only as a matter of method.

her desire is disguised in anxiety or is contested by fear, we should regard as an original fact this blending of urgency and apprehension which is female desire: it is the indissoluble synthesis of attraction and repulsion that characterizes it. We note that many female animals avoid copulation even as they are soliciting it, and we are tempted to accuse them of coquetry or hypocrisy ; but it is absurd to pretend to explain primitive behaviour patterns by asserting their similarity to complex modes of conduct. On the contrary, the former are in truth at the source of the attitudes that in woman are called coquetry and hypocrisy. The notion of a 'passive libido' is baffling, since the libido has been defined, on the basis of the male, as a drive, an energy ; but one would do no better to hold the opinion that a light could be at once yellow and blue —what is needed is the intuition of green. We would more fully encompass reality if instead of defining the libido in vague terms of 'energy' we brought the significance of sexuality into relation with that of other human attitudes—taking, capturing, eating, making, submitting, and so forth ; for it is one of the various modes of apprehending an object. We should study also the qualities of the erotic object as it presents itself not only in the sexual act but also to observation in general. Such an investigation extends beyond the frame of psychoanalysis, which assumes eroticism as irreducible.

Furthermore, I shall pose the problem of feminine destiny quite otherwise: I shall place woman in a world of values and give her behaviour a dimension of liberty. I believe that she has the power to choose between the assertion of her transcendence and her alienation as object ; she is not the plaything of contradictory drives ; she devises solutions of diverse values in the ethical scale. Replacing value with authority, choice with drive, psychoanalysis offers an *Ersatz,* a substitute, for morality—the concept of normality. This concept is certainly most useful in therapeutics, but it has spread through psychoanalysis in general to a disquieting extent. The descriptive schema is proposed as a law ; and most assuredly a mechanistic psychology cannot accept the notion of moral invention ; it can in strictness render an account of the *less* and never of the more ; in strictness it can admit of checks, never of creations. If a subject does not show in his totality the development considered as normal, it will be said that his development has been arrested, and this arrest will be interpreted as a lack, a negation, but never as a positive decision. This it is, among other things, that makes the psychoanalysis of great men so shocking: we are told that such and such a transference, this or that sublimation, has not taken place in them; it is not suggested that perhaps they have refused to undergo the process, perhaps for good reasons of their own; it is not thought desirable to regard their behaviour as possibly motivated by purposes freely envisaged; the individual is always explained through ties with his past and not in respect to a future towards which he projects his aims. Thus the psychoanalysts never give us more than an inauthentic picture, and for the inauthentic there can hardly be found any other criterion than normality. Their statement of the feminine destiny is absolutely to the point in this connection. In the sense in which the psychoanalysts understand the term, 'to identify oneself' with the mother or with the father is to *alienate oneself* in a model, it is to prefer a foreign image to the spontaneous manifestation of one's own existence, it is to play at being. Woman is shown to us as enticed by two modes of alienation. Evidently to play at being a man will be for her a source of frustration; but to play at being a woman is also a delusion: to be a woman would mean to be the object, the *Other*—and the Other nevertheless remains subject in the midst of her resignation.

The true problem for woman is to reject these flights from reality and seek self-fulfilment in transcendence. The thing to do, then, is to see what possibilities are opened up for her through what are called the virile and the feminine attitudes. When a child takes the road indicated by one or the other of its parents, it may be because the child freely takes up their projects; its behaviour may be the result of a choice motivated by ends and aims. Even with Adler the will to power is only an absurd kind of energy; he denominates as 'masculine protest' every project involving transcendence. When a little girl climbs trees it is, according to Adler, just to show her equality with boys; it does not occur to him that she likes to climb trees. For the mother her child is something quite other than an 'equivalent of the penis'. To paint, to write, to engage in politics—these are not merely 'sublimations'; here we have aims that are willed for their own sakes. To deny it is to falsify all human history.

The reader will note a certain parallelism between this account and that of the psychoanalysts. The fact is that from the male point of view—which is adopted by both male and female psychoanalysts—behaviour involving alienation is regarded as feminine, that in which the subject asserts his transcendence **as** virile. Donaldson, a historian of woman, remarked that the definitions: 'man is a male human being, woman is a female human being', have been asymmetrically distorted; and it is among the psychoanalysts in particular that man is defined as a human being and woman as a female —whenever she behaves as a human being she is said to imitate the male. The psychoanalyst describes the female child, the young girl, as incited to identification with the mother and the father, torn between 'viriloid' and 'feminine' tendencies; whereas I conceive her as hesitating between the role of *object, Other* which is offered her, and the assertion of her liberty. Thus it is that we shall agree on a certain number of facts, especially when we take up the avenues of inauthentic flight open to women. But we accord them by no means the same significance as does the Freudian or the Adlerian. For us woman is defined as a human being in quest of values in a world of values, a world of which it is indispensable to know the economic and social structure. We shall study woman in an existential perspective with due regard to her total situation.

CHAPTER III

THE POINT OF VIEW OF HISTORICAL MATERIALISM

THE theory of historical materialism has brought to light some most important truths. Humanity is not an animal species, it is a historical reality. Human society is an antiphysis—in a sense it is against nature; it does not passively submit to the presence of nature but rather takes over the control of nature on its own behalf. This arrogation is not an inward, subjective operation; it is accomplished objectively in practical action.

Thus woman could not be considered simply as a sexual organism, for among the biological traits, only those have importance that take on concrete value in action. Woman's awareness of herself is not defined exclusively by her sexuality: it reflects a situation that depends upon the economic organization of society, which in turn indicates what stage of technical evolution mankind has attained. As we have seen, the two essential traits that characterize woman, biologically speaking, are the following: her grasp upon the world is less extended than man's, and she is more closely enslaved to the species.

But these facts take on quite different values according to the economic and social context. In human history grasp upon the world has never been defined by the naked body: the hand, with its opposable thumb, already anticipates the instrument that multiplies its power; from the most ancient records of prehistory, we see man always as armed. In times when heavy clubs were brandished and wild beasts held at bay, woman's physical weakness did constitute a glaring inferiority: if the instrument required strength slightly beyond that at woman's disposal, it was enough to make her appear utterly powerless. But, on the contrary, technique may annul the muscular inequality of man and woman: abundance makes for superiority only in the perspective of a need, and to have too much is no better than to have enough. Thus the control of many modern machines requires only a part of the masculine resources, and if the minimum demanded is not above the female's capacity, she becomes, as far as this work is concerned, man's equal. Today, of course, vast displays of energy can be controlled by pressing a button. As for the burdens of maternity, they assume widely varying importance according to the customs of the country: they are crushing if the woman is obliged to undergo frequent pregnancies and if she is compelled to nurse and raise the children without assistance; but if she procreates voluntarily and if society comes to her aid during pregnancy and is concerned with child welfare, the burdens of maternity are light and can be easily offset by suitable adjustments in working conditions.

Engels retraces the history of woman according to this perspective in *The Origin of the Family, Private Property, and the State*, showing that this history depended essentially on that of techniques. In the Stone Age, when the land belonged in common to all members of the clan, the rudimentary character of the primitive spade and hoe limited the possibilities of agriculture, so that woman's strength was adequate for gardening. In this primitive division of labour, the two sexes constituted in a way two classes, and there was equality between these classes. While man hunts and fishes, woman remains in the home; but the tasks of domesticity include productive labour—making pottery, weaving, gardening—and in consequence woman plays a large part in economic life. Through the discovery of copper, tin, bronze, and iron, and with the appearance of the plough, agriculture enlarges its scope, and intensive labour is called for in clearing woodland and cultivating the fields. Then man has recourse to the labour of other men, whom he reduces to slavery. Private property appears: master of slaves and of the earth, man becomes the proprietor also of woman. This was 'the great historical defeat of the feminine sex'. It is to be explained by the upsetting of the old division of labour which occurred in consequence of the invention of new tools. 'The same cause which had assured to woman the prime authority in the house—namely, her restriction to domestic duties—this same cause now assured the domination there of the man; for woman's housework henceforth sank into insignificance in comparison with man's productive labour—the latter was everything, the former a trifling auxiliary.' Then maternal authority gave place to paternal authority, property being inherited from father to son and no longer from woman to her clan. Here we see the emergence of the patriarchal family
76

founded upon private property. In this type of family woman is subjugated. Man in his sovereignty indulges himself in sexual caprices, among others—he fornicates with slaves or courtesans or he practises polygamy. Wherever the local customs make reciprocity at all possible, the wife takes revenge through infidelity—marriage finds its natural fulfilment in adultery. This is woman's sole defence against the domestic slavery in which she is bound ; and it is this economic oppression that gives rise to the social oppression to which she is subjected. Equality cannot be re-established until the two sexes enjoy equal rights in law ; but this enfranchisement requires participation in general industry by the whole female sex. 'Woman can be emancipated only when she can take part on a large social scale in production and is engaged in domestic work only to an insignificant degree. And this has become possible only in the big industry of modern times, which not only admits of female labour on a grand scale but even formally demands it. . . .'

Thus the fate of woman and that of socialism are intimately bound up together, as is shown also in Bebel's great work on woman. 'Woman and the proletariat,' he says, 'are both downtrodden.' Both are to be set free through the economic development consequent upon the social upheaval brought about by machinery. The problem of woman is reduced to the problem of her capacity for labour. Puissant at the time when techniques were suited to her capabilites, dethroned when she was no longer in a position to exploit them, woman regains in the modern world her equality with man. It is the resistance of the ancient capitalistic paternalism that in most countries prevents the concrete realization of this equality ; it will be realized on the day when this resistance is broken, as is the fact already in the Soviet Union, according to Soviet propaganda. And when the socialist society is established throughout the world, there will no longer be men and women, but only workers on a footing of equality.

Although this chain of thought as outlined by Engels marks an advance upon those we have been examining, we find it disappointing—the most important problems are slurred over. The turning-point of all history is the passage from the regime of community ownership to that of private property, and it is in no wise indicated how this could have come about. Engels himself declares in *The Origin of the Family* that 'at present we know nothing about it' ; not only is he ignorant of the historical details: he does not even suggest any interpretation. Similarly, it is not clear that the institution of private property must necessarily have involved the enslavement of women. Historical materialism takes for granted facts that call for explanation: Engels assumes without discussion the bond of *interest* which ties man to property ; but where does this interest, the source of social institutions, have its own source? Thus Engels's account remains superficial, and the truths that he does reveal are seemingly contingent, incidental. The fact is that we cannot plumb their meaning without going beyond the limits of historical materialism. It cannot provide solutions for the problems we have raised, because these concern the whole man and not that abstraction: *Homo oeconomicus.*

It would seem clear, for example, that the very concept of personal possession can be comprehensible only with reference to the original condition of the existent. For it to appear, there must have been at first an inclination in the subject to think of himself as basically individual, to assert the autonomy and separateness of his existence. We can see that this affirmation would have remained subjective, inward, without validity as long as the individual lacked the practical means for carrying it out objectively. Without adequate tools, he did not sense at first any power over the world, he felt lost in nature and in the group, passive, threatened, the plaything of obscure forces ; he dared think of himself only as identified with the clan: the totem, mana, the earth were group realities. The discovery of bronze enabled man, in the experience of hard and productive labour, to discover himself as creator ; dominating nature, he was no longer afraid of it, and in the fact of obstacles overcome he found courage to see himself as an autonomous active force, to achieve self-fulfilment as an individual.[1] But this accomplishment would never have been attained had not man originally willed it so ; the lesson of work is not inscribed upon a passive subject: the subject shapes and masters himself in shaping and mastering the land.

On the other hand, the affirmation of the subject's individu-

[1] GASTON BACHELARD in *La Terre et les rêveries de la volonté* makes among others a suggestive study of the blacksmith. He shows how man, through the hammer and the anvil, asserts himself and his individuality. 'The blacksmith's instant is an instant at once well marked off and magnified. It promotes the worker to the mastery of time, through the forcefulness of an instant' (p. 142); and farther on : 'The man at the forge accepts the challenge of the universe arrayed against him.'

ality is not enough to explain property: each conscious individual through challenge, struggle, and single combat can endeavour to raise himself to sovereignty. For the challenge to have taken the form of *potlatch* or ceremonial exchange of gifts—that is, of an economic rivalry—and from this point on for first the chief and then the members of the clan to have laid claim to private property, required that there should be in man another original tendency. As we have seen in the preceding chapter, the existent succeeds in finding himself only in estrangement, in alienation; he seeks through the world to find himself in some shape, other than himself, which he makes his own. The clan encounters its own alienated existence in the totem, the mana, the terrain it occupies; and when the individual becomes distinguished from the community, he requires a personal incarnation. The mana becomes individualized in the chief, then in each individual; and at the same time each person tries to appropriate a piece of land, implements, crops. Man finds himself in these goods which are his because he has previously lost himself in them; and it is therefore understandable that he places upon them a value no less fundamental than upon his very life. Thus it is that man's *interest* in his property becomes an intelligible relation. But we see that this cannot be explained through the tool alone: we must grasp in its entirety the attitude of man wielding the tool, an attitude that implies an ontological substructure, a foundation in the nature of his being.

On the same grounds it is impossible to *deduce* the oppression of woman from the institution of private property. Here again the inadequacy of Engels's pont of view is obvious. He saw clearly that woman's muscular weakness became a real point of inferiority only in its relation to the bronze and iron tool; but he did not see that the limitations of her capacity for labour constituted in themselves a concrete disadvantage only in a certain perspective. It is because man is a being of transcendence and ambition that he projects new urgencies through every new tool: when he had invented bronze implements, he was no longer content with gardens—he wanted to clear and cultivate vast fields. And it was not from the bronze itself that this desire welled up. Woman's incapacity brought about her ruin because man regarded her in the perspectiveness of his project for enrichment and expansion. And this project is still not enough to explain why she was oppressed; for the division of labour between the sexes could have meant a friendly association. If the original relation

79

between a man and his fellows was exclusively a relation of friendship, we could not account for any type of enslavement; but no, this phenomenon is a result of the imperialism of the human consciousness, seeking always to exercise its sovereignty in objective fashion. If the human consciousness had not included the original category of the Other and an original aspiration to dominate the Other, the invention of the bronze tool could not have caused the oppression of woman.

No more does Engels account for the peculiar nature of this oppression. He tried to reduce the antagonism of the sexes to class conflict, but he was half-hearted in the attempt; the thesis is simply untenable. It is true that division of labour according to sex and the consequent oppression bring to mind in some ways the division of society by classes, but it is impossible to confuse the two. For one thing, there is no biological basis for the separation of classes. Again, the slave in his toil is conscious of himself as opposed to his master; and the proletariat has always put its condition to the test in revolt, thereby going back to essentials and constituting a threat to its exploiters. And what it has aimed at is its own disappearance as a class. I have pointed out in the Introduction how different woman's situation is, particularly on account of the community of life and interests which entails her solidarity with man, and also because he finds in her an accomplice; no desire for revolution dwells within her, nor any thought of her own disappearance as a sex—all she asks is that certain sequels of sexual differentiation be abolished.

What is still more serious, woman cannot in good faith be regarded simply as a worker; for her reproductive function is as important as her productive capacity, no less in the social economy than in the individual life. In some periods, indeed, it is more useful to produce offspring than to plough the soil. Engels slighted the problem, simply remarking that the socialist community would abolish the family—certainly an abstract solution. We know how often and how radically Soviet Russia has had to change its policy on the family according to the varying relation between the immediate needs of production and those of re-population. But for that matter, to do away with the family is not necessarily to emancipate woman. Such examples as Sparta and the Nazi regime prove that she can be none the less oppressed by the males, for all her direct attachment to the State.

A truly socialist ethics, concerned to uphold justice without suppressing liberty and to impose duties upon individuals without abolishing individuality, will find most embarrassing the problems posed by the condition of woman. It is impossible to equate gestation with a *task*, a piece of work, or with a *service*, such as military service. Woman's life is more seriously broken upon by a demand for children than by regulation of the citizen's employment—no state has ever ventured to establish obligatory copulation. In the sexual act and in maternity not only time and strength but also essential values are involved for woman. Rationalist materialism tries in vain to disregard this dramatic aspect of sexuality ; for it is impossible to bring the sexual instinct under a code of regulations. Indeed, as Freud said, it is not sure that it does not bear within itself a denial of its own satisfaction. What is certain is that it does not permit of integration with the social, because there is in eroticism a revolt of the instant against time, of the individual against the universal. In proposing to direct and exploit it, there is risk of killing it, for it is impossible to deal at will with living spontaneity as one deals at will with inert matter ; and no more can it be obtained by force, as a privilege may be.

There is no way of directly compelling woman to bring forth : all that can be done is to put her in a situation where maternity is for her the sole outcome—the law or the mores enjoin marriage, birth control and abortion are prohibited, divorce is forbidden. These ancient patriarchal restraints are just what Soviet Russia has brought back today ; Russia has revived the paternalistic concepts of marriage. And in doing so, she has been induced to ask woman once more to make of herself an erotic object : in a recent pronouncement female Soviet citizens were requested to pay careful attention to their garb, to use make-up, to employ the arts of coquetry in holding their husbands and fanning the flame of desire. As this case shows clearly, it is impossible to regard woman simply as a productive force : she is for man a sexual partner, a reproducer, an erotic object—an Other through whom he seeks himself. In vain have the totalitarian or authoritative regimes with one accord prohibited psychoanalysis and declared that individual, personal drama is out of order for citizens loyally integrated with the community ; the erotic experience remains one in which generality is always regained by an individuality. And for a democratic socialism in which classes are abolished but not individuals, the question of individual destiny would keep all its importance—and hence sexual differentiation

81

would keep all its importance. The sexual relation that joins woman to man is not the same as that which he bears to her ; and the bond that unites her to the child is *sui generis,* unique. She was not created by the bronze tool alone ; and the machine alone will not abolish her. To claim for her every right, every chance to be an all-round human being does not mean that we should be blind to her peculiar situation. And in order to comprehend that situation we must look beyond the historical materialism that perceives in man and woman no more than economic units.

So it is that we reject for the same reasons both the sexual monism of Freud and the economic monism of Engels. A psychoanalyst will interpret all social claims of woman as phenomena of the 'masculine protest' ; for the Marxist, on the contrary, her sexuality only expresses her economic situation in more or less complex, roundabout fashion. But the categories of 'clitorid' and 'vaginal', like the categories of 'bourgeois' or 'proletarian', are equally inadequate to encompass a concrete woman. Underlying all individual drama, as it underlies the economic history of mankind, there is an existentialist foundation that alone enables us to understand in its unity that particular form of being which we call a human life. The virtue of Freudianism derives from the fact that the existent is a body: what he experiences as a body confronted by other bodies expresses his existential situation concretely. Similarly, what is true in the Marxian thesis is that the ontological aspirations—the projects for becoming— of the existent take concrete form according to the material possibilities offered, especially those opened up by technological advances. But unless they are integrated into the totality of human reality, sexuality and technology alone can explain nothing. That is why in Freud the prohibitions of the super- ego and the drives of the ego appear to be contingent, and why in Engels's account of the history of the family the most important developments seem to arise according to the caprices of mysterious fortune. In our attempt to discover woman we shall not reject certain contributions of biology, of psycho- analysis, and of historical materialism ; but we shall hold that the body, the sexual life, and the resources of technology exist concretely for man only in so far as he grasps them in the total perspective of his existence. The value of muscu- lar strength, of the phallus, of the tool can be defined only in a world of values ; it is determined by the basic project through which the existent seeks transcendence.

PART II

HISTORY

CHAPTER I

THE NOMADS

T H I S has always been a man's world; and none of the reasons hitherto brought forward in explanation of this fact has seemed adequate. But we shall be able to understand how the hierarchy of the sexes was established by reviewing the data of prehistoric research and ethnography in the light of existentialist philosophy. I have already stated that when two human categories are together, each aspires to impose its sovereignty upon the other. If both are able to resist this imposition, there is created between them a reciprocal relation, sometimes in amity, always in a state of tension. If one of the two is in some way privileged, has some advantage, this one prevails over the other and undertakes to keep it in subjection. It is therefore understandable that man would wish to dominate woman; but what advantage has enabled him to carry out his will?

The accounts of the primitive forms of human society provided by ethnographers are extremely contradictory, the more so as they are better informed and less systematized. It is peculiarly difficult to form an idea of woman's situation in the pre-agricultural period. We do not even know whether woman's musculature or her respiratory apparatus, under conditions different from those of today, were not as well developed as in man. She had hard work to do, and in particular it was she who carried the burdens. The last fact is of doubtful significance; it is likely that if she was assigned this function, it was because a man kept his hands free on the trail in order to defend himself against possible aggressors, animal or human; his role was the more dangerous and the one that demanded more vigour. It would appear, nevertheless, that in many cases the women were strong and tough enough to take part in the warriors' expeditions. We need recall only the tales of Herodotus and the more recent accounts of the amazons of Dahomey to realize that woman has shared in warfare—and with no less ferocity and cruelty than man; but even so, man's superior strength must have been of tremendous importance in the age of the club and the wild beast. In any case, however strong the women were, the bondage of reproduction was a terrible handicap in the struggle against a hostile world. Pregnancy, childbirth, and menstruation reduced their capacity for work and made them at times wholly dependent upon the men for protection and food. As there was obviously no birth control, and as nature failed to provide women with sterile periods like other mammalian females, closely spaced maternities must have absorbed most of their strength and their time, so that they were incapable of providing for the children they brought into the world. Here we have a first fact heavily freighted with consequences: the early days of the human species were difficult; the gathering, hunting, and fishing peoples got only meagre products from the soil and those with great effort; too many children were born for the group's resources; the extravagant fertility of woman prevented her from active participation in the increase of these resources while she created new needs to an indefinite extent. Necessary as she was for the perpetuation of the species, she perpetuated it too generously, and so it was the man who had to assure equilibrium between reproduction and production. Even in times when humanity most needed births, when maternity was most venerated, manual labour was the primary necessity, and woman was never permitted to take first place. The primitive hordes had no permanence in property or territory, and hence set no store by posterity; children were for them a burden, not a prized possession. Infanticide was common among the nomads, and many of the newborn that escaped massacre died from lack of care in the general state of indifference.

The woman who gave birth, therefore, did not know the pride of creation; she felt herself the plaything of obscure forces, and the painful ordeal of childbirth seemed a useless or even troublesome accident. But in any case giving birth and suckling are not *activities,* they are natural functions; no project is involved; and that is why woman found in them ne reason for a lofty affirmation of her existence—she submitted passively to her biologic fate. The domestic labours that fell to her lot because they were reconcilable with the cares of maternity imprisoned her in repetition and

86

immanence;[1] they were repeated from day to day in an identical form, which was perpetuated almost without change from century to century; they produced nothing new.

Man's case was radically different; he furnished support for the group, not in the manner of worker bees by a simple vital process, through biological behaviour, but by means of acts that transcended his animal nature. *Homo faber* has from the beginning of time been an inventor: and the stick and the club with which he armed himself to knock down fruits and to slaughter animals became forthwith instruments for enlarging his grasp upon the world. He did not limit himself to bringing home the fish he caught in the sea: first he had to conquer the watery realm by means of the dugout fashioned from a tree-trunk; to get at the riches of the world he annexed the world itself. In this activity he put his power to the test; he set up goals and opened up roads towards them; in brief, he found self-realization as an existent. To maintain, he created; he burst out of the present, he opened the future. This is the reason why fishing and hunting expeditions had a sacred character. Their successes were celebrated with festivals and triumphs, and therein man gave recognition to his human estate. Today he still manifests this pride when he has built a dam or a skyscraper or an atomic pile. He has worked not merely to conserve the world as given; he has broken through its frontiers, he has laid down the foundations of a new future.

Early man's activity had another dimension that gave it supreme dignity; it was often dangerous. If blood were but a nourishing fluid, it would be valued no higher than milk; but the hunter was no butcher, for in the struggle against wild animals he ran great risks. The warrior put his life in jeopardy to elevate the prestige of the horde, the clan to which he belonged. And in this he proved dramatically that life is not the supreme value for man, but on the contrary that it should be made to serve ends more important than itself. The worst curse that was laid upon woman was that she should be excluded from these warlike forays. For it is not in giving life but in risking life that man is raised above the animal; that is why superiority has been accorded in

[1] This word, frequently used by the author, always signifies, as here, the opposite or negation of transcendence, such as confinement or restriction to a narrow round of uncreative and repetitious duties; it is in contrast to the freedom to engage in projects of ever widening scope that marks the untrammelled existent.—TR.

humanity not to the sex that brings forth but to that which kills.

Here we have the key to the whole mystery. On the biological level a species is maintained only by creating itself anew ; but this creation results only in repeating the same Life in more individuals. But man assures the repetition of Life while transcending Life through Existence ; by this transcendence he creates values that deprive pure repetition of all value. In the animal, the freedom and variety of male activities are vain because no project is involved. Except for his services to the species, what he does is immaterial. Whereas in serving the species, the human male also remodels the face of the earth, he creates new instruments, he invents, he shapes the future. In setting himself up as sovereign, he is supported by the complicity of woman herself. For she, too, is an existent, she feels the urge to surpass, and her project is not mere repetition but transcendence towards a different future—in her heart of hearts she finds confirmation of the masculine pretensions. She joins the men in the festivals that celebrate the successes and the victories of the males. Her misfortune is to have been biologically destines for the repetition of Life, when even in her own view Life does not carry within itself its reasons for being, reasons that are more important than the life itself.

Certain passages in the argument employed by Hegel in defining the relation of master to slave apply much better to the relation of man to woman. The advantage of the master, he says, comes from his affirmation of Spirit as against Life through the fact that he risks his own life ; but in fact the conquered slave has known this same risk. Whereas woman is basically an existent who gives Life and does not risk *her* life ; between her and the male there has been no combat. Hegel's definition would seem to apply especially well to her. He says : 'The other consciousness is the dependent consciousness for whom the essential reality is the animal type of life ; that is to say, a mode of living bestowed by another entity.' But this relation is to be distinguished from the relation of subjugation because woman also aspires to and recognizes the values that are concretely attained by the male. He it is who opens up the future to which she also reaches out. In truth women have never set up female values in opposition to male values ; it is man who, desirous of maintaining masculine prerogatives, has invented that divergence. Men have presumed to create a feminine domain—the kingdom of life, of immanence—only in order to lock up women therein. But it is regardless of sex that the existent seeks self-justification through transcendence—the very submission of women is proof of that statement. What they demand today is to be recognized as existents by the same right as men and not to subordinate existence to life, the human being to its animality.

An existentialist perspective has enabled us, then, to understand how the biological and economic condition of the primitive horde must have led to male supremacy. The female, to a greater extent than the male, is the prey of the species; and the human race has always sought to escape its specific destiny. The support of life became for man an activity and a project through the invention of the tool; but in maternity woman remained closely bound to her body, like an animal. It is because humanity calls itself in question in the matter of living—that is to say, values the reasons for living above mere life—that, confronting woman, man assumes mastery. Man's design is not to repeat himself in time: it is to take control of the instant and mould the future. It is male activity that in creating values has made of existence itself a value; this activity has prevailed over the confused forces of life; it has subdued Nature and Woman. We must now see how this situation has been perpetuated and how it has evolved through the ages. What place has humanity made for this portion of itself which, while included within it, is defined as the Other? What rights have been conceded to it? How have men defined it?

CHAPTER II

EARLY TILLERS OF THE SOIL

W E have just seen that woman's lot was a very hard one in the primitive horde, and doubtless there was no great effort made to compensate for the cruel disadvantages that handicapped woman. But neither was woman put upon and bullied as happened later under paternalistic auspices. No institution ratified the inequality of the sexes; indeed, there were no institutions—no property, no inheritance, no jurisprudence. Religion was neuter: worship was offered to some asexual totem.

Institutions and the law appeared when the nomads settled down on the land and became agriculturists. Man no longer limited himself to harsh combat against hostile forces; he began to express himself through the shape he imposed upon the world, to think of the world and of himself. At this point the sexual differentiation was reflected in the structure of the human group, and it took on a special form. In agricultural communities woman was often clothed in extraordinary prestige. This prestige is to be explained essentially by the quite new importance that the child acquired in a civilization based on working the soil. In settling down on a certain territory, men established ownership of it, and property appeared in a collectivized form. This property required that its possessors provide a posterity, and maternity became a sacred function.

Many tribes lived under a communal regime, but this does not mean that the women belonged to all the men in common —it is hardly held today that promiscuity was ever the general practice—but men and women experienced religious, social, and economic existence only as a group: their individuality remained a purely biological fact. Marriage, whatever its form—monogamy, polygamy, or polyandry—was only a secular accident, creating no mystical tie. It involved no servitude for the wife, for she was still integrated with her clan. The whole body of a clan, unified under a single totem, possessed in a mystical sense a single mana, materially the common enjoyment of a single territory. According to the process of alienation I have already discussed, the clan found self-awareness in this territory under an objective and concrete form; through the permanence of the land, therefore, the clan became a real unity, whose identity persisted through the passage of time.

This existentialist position alone enables us to understand the identification that has existed up to the present time between the clan, the tribe, or the family, and property. In place of the outlook of the nomadic tribes, living only for the moment, the agricultural community substituted the concept of a life rooted in the past and connected with the future. Veneration was accorded to the totemic ancestor who gave his name to the members of the clan; and the clan took a profound interest in its own descendants, for it would achieve survival through the land that it would bequeath to them and that they would exploit. The community sensed its unity and desired a continued existence beyond the present; it recognized itself in its children, recognized them as its own; and in them it found fulfilment and transcendence.

Now, many primitive peoples were ignorant of the part taken by the father in the procreation of children (and in a few cases this seems to be true even today); they regarded children as the reincarnation of ancestral spirits that hover about certain trees or rocks, in certain sacred places, and come down and enter the bodies of women. Sometimes it was held that the woman ought not to be a virgin, so as to permit this infiltration; but other peoples believed that it could occur as well through the nostrils or the mouth. In any case, defloration was secondary in the matter, and for reasons of a mystical nature it was rarely the prerogative of the husband.

But the mother was obviously necessary for the birth of the child; she it was who protected and nourished the germ within her body, and therefore it was through her that the life of the clan in the visible world was propagated. Thus she came to play a role of the first importance. Very often the children belonged to their mother's clan, carried its name, and shared its rights and privileges, particularly in the use of the land held by the clan. Communal property was handed down by the women: through them ownership in the fields and harvests was assured to members of the clan, and conversely these members were destined through their mothers for this or that domain. We may suppose, then, that in a mystical sense the earth belonged to the women: they had a hold, at once religious and legal, upon the land and its fruits. The tie between woman and land was still closer than that of ownership, for the matrilineal regime was characterized by a veritable assimilation of woman to the earth ; in both the permanence of life—which is essentially generation—was accomplished through the reproduction of its individual embodiments, its avatars.

Among the nomads procreation seemed hardly more than accidental, and the wealth of the soil remained unknown ; but the husbandman marvelled at the mystery of the fecundity that burgeoned in his furrows and in the maternal body : he realized that he had been engendered like the cattle and the crops, he wanted his clan to engender other men who would perpetuate it while perpetuating the fertility of the fields ; all nature seemed to him like a mother : the land is woman and in woman abide the same dark powers as in the earth.[1] It was for this reason in part that agricultural labour was entrusted to woman ; able to summon ancestral spirits into her body, she would also have power to cause fruits and grain to spring up from the planted fields. In both cases there was no question of a creative act, but of a magic conjuration. At this stage man no longer limited himself to gathering the products of the soil, but he did not as yet know his power. He stood hesitant between technique and magic, feeling himself passive, dependent upon Nature, which dealt out life and death at random. To be sure, he realized more or less clearly the effectiveness of the sexual act and of the techniques by which he brought the land under cultivation. Yet children and crops seemed none the less to be gifts of the gods, and the mysterious emanations from the female body were believed to bring into this world the riches latent in the mysterious sources of life.

Such beliefs are still deep-rooted and are alive today in many Indian, Australian, and Polynesian tribes. In some a sterile woman is considered dangerous for the garden, in others it is thought that the harvest will be more abundant if it is gathered by a pregnant woman ; in India naked women formerly pushed the plough around the field at night, and so on. These beliefs and customs have always taken on all the more importance because they harmonized with the practical interests of the community. Maternity dooms woman to a

[1] 'Hail, Earth, mother of men, may you be fertile in the embrace of God and may you be filled with fruits for man's use,' says an old Anglo-Saxon incantation.

sedentary existence, and so it is natural that she remain at the hearth while man hunts, goes fishing, and makes war. But among primitive peoples the gardens were small and located within the village limits, and their cultivation was a domestic task ; the use of Stone Age tools demanded no great strength. Economics and religion were at one in leaving agricultural labour to the women. As domestic industry developed, it also was their lot: they wove mattings and blankets and they made pottery. Frequently they took charge of barter ; commerce was in their hands. Through them, therefore, the life of the clan was maintained and extended ; children, flocks, crops, utensils, all the prosperity of the group, depended on their labour and their magic powers—they were the soul of the community. Such powers inspired in men a respect mingled with fear, which was reflected in their worship. In woman was to be summed up the whole of alien Nature.

As I have already said, man never thinks of himself without thinking of the Other ; he views the world under the sign of duality, which is not in the first place sexual in character. But being different from man, who sets himself up as the same, it is naturally to the category of the Other that woman is consigned ; the Other includes woman. At first she is not of sufficient importance to incarnate the Other all by herself, and so a sub-division is apparent at the heart of the Other: in the ancient cosmogonies a single element often has an incarnation that is at once male and female ; thus the Ocean (male) and the Sea (feminine) are for the ancient Babylonians the double incarnation of cosmic chaos. When woman's role enlarges, she comes to represent almost in its entirety the region of the Other. Then appear those feminine divinities through whom the idea of fecundity is worshipped. At Susa was found the oldest figure of the Great Goddess, the Great Mother with long robe and high coiffure whom in other statues we see crowned with towers. The excavations in Crete have yielded several such images. She is at times steatopygous and crouching, at times slender and standing erect, sometimes dressed and often naked, her arms pressed beneath her swelling breasts. She is the queen of heaven, a dove her symbol ; she is also the empress of hell, whence she crawls forth, symbolized in a serpent. She is made manifest in the mountains and the woods, on the sea, and in springs of water. Everywhere she creates life ; if she kills, she also revives the dead. Capricious, luxurious, cruel as

Nature, at once propitious and fearsome, she reigns over all the Aegean Archipelago, over Phrygia, Syria, Anatolia, over all western Asia. She is called Ishtar in Babylonia, Astarte among Semitic peoples, and Gaea, Rhea, or Cybele by the Greeks. In Egypt we come upon her under the form of Isis. Male divinities are subordinated to her.

Supreme idol in the far realms of heaven and hell, woman is on earth surrounded with taboos like all sacred beings, she is herself taboo ; because of the powers she holds, she is looked upon as a magician, a sorceress. She is invoked in prayers, sometimes she becomes a priestess as with the Druids among the ancient Celts. In certain instances she takes part in tribal government, and may even become sole ruler. These remote ages have bequeathed to us no literature. But the great patriarchal epochs preserved in their mythology, their monuments, and their traditions the memory of the times when woman occupied a very lofty situation. From the feminine point of vew, the Brahmanic epoch shows regression from that of the *Rig-Veda,* and the latter from that of the preceding primitive stage. Bedouin women of the pre-Islamic period enjoyed a status quite superior to that assigned them by the Koran. The great figures of Niobe, of Medea, evoke an era in which mothers took pride in their children, regarding them as treasures peculiarly their own. And in Homer's poems Andromache and Hecuba had an importance that classic Greece no longer attributed to women hidden in the shadows of the gynaeceum.

These facts have led to the supposition that in primitive times a veritable reign of women existed: the matriarchy. It was this hypothesis, proposed by Bachofen, that Engels adopted, regarding the passage from the matriarchate to the patriarchate as 'the great historical defeat of the feminine sex'. But in truth that Golden Age of Woman is only a myth. To say that woman was the *Other* is to say that there did not exist between the sexes a reciprocal relation: Earth, Mother, Goddess—she was no fellow creature in man's eyes ; it was *beyond* the human realm that her power was affirmed, and she was therefore *outside* of that realm. Society has always been male ; political power has always been in the hands of men. 'Public or simply social authority always belongs to men,' declares Lévi-Strauss at the end of his study of primitive societies.

For the male it is always another male who is the fellow being, the other who is also the same, with whom reciprocal relations **are** established. The duality that appears within societies under one form or another opposes a group of men to a group of men ; women constitute a part of the property which each of these groups possesses and which is a medium of exchange between them. The mistake has come from a confusion of two forms of alterity or otherness, which are mutually exclusive in point of fact. To the precise degree in which woman is regarded as the absolute Other—that is to say, whatever her magic powers, as the inessential—it is to that degree impossible to consider her as another subject.[1] Women, therefore, have never composed a separate group set up *on its own account* over against the male grouping. They have never entered into a direct and autonomous relation with the men. 'The reciprocal bond basic to marriage is not set up between men and women, but between men and men by means of women, who are only the principal occasion for it,' says Lévi-Strauss.[2] The actual condition of woman has not been affected by the type of filiation (mode of tracing descent) that prevails in the society to which she belongs ; whether the system be patrilineal, matrilineal, bilateral, or non-differentiated (the non-differentiation never being strictly adhered to), she is always under the guardianship of the males. The only question is whether the woman after marriage will remain subject to the authority of her father or of her older brother—an authority that will extend also to her children—or whether she will become subject to that of her husband. 'Woman, in herself, is never more than the symbol of her line . . . matrilineal filiation is but the authority of the woman's father or brother, which extends back to the brother's village,' to quote Lévi-Strauss again. She is only the intermediary of authority, not the one who holds it. The fact is that the relations of two groups of men are defined by the system of filiation, and not the relation between the two sexes.

In practice the actual condition of woman is not bound up with this or that type of authority. It may happen that in the

---

[1] This discrimination, as we shall see, has been perpetuated. The epochs that have regarded woman as the Other are those which refuse most harshly to integrate her with society by right of being human. Today she can become an *other* who is also an equal only in losing her mystic aura. The anti-feminists have always played upon this equivocation. They are glad to exalt woman as the *Other* in such a manner as to make her alterity absolute, irreducible, and to deny her access to the human *Mitsein*.

[2] *Les Structures élémentaires de la parenté.*

matrilineal system she has a very high position; still, we must be careful to note that the presence of a woman chief or queen at the head of a tribe by no means signifies that women are sovereign therein: the accession to the throne of Catherine the Great in no way modified the lot of the Russian peasant women; and it is no less frequent for her to live in an abject condition. Furthermore, the cases are very rare in which the wife remains living with her clan, her husband being permitted only hasty, even clandestine visits. Almost always she goes to live under her husband's roof, a fact that is enough to show the primacy of the male. 'Behind the shifting modes of filiation,' writes Lévi-Strauss, 'the persistence of the patrilocal residence bears witness to the fundamentally asymmetrical relation between the sexes that marks human society.' Since woman keeps her children with her, the result is that the territorial organization of the tribe does not correspond with its totemic organization—the former is dependent on circumstances, contingent; the latter is rigorously established. But practically the first has the more importance, for the place where people live and work counts more than their mystical connection.

In the more widespread transitional regimes there are two kinds of authority which interlock, the one religious, the other based on the occupation and working of the land. For being only a secular institution, marriage has none the less a great social importance, and the conjugal family, although stripped of religious significance, has a vigorous life on the human plane. Even in groups where great sexual freedom exists, it is proper for the woman who brings a child into the world to be married; she is unable to form an autonomous group, alone with her progeny. And the religious protection of her brother is insufficient: the presence of a spouse is required. He often has heavy responsibilities in regard to his children. They do not belong to his clan, but nevertheless it is he who must provide for them and bring them up. Between husband and wife, father and son, are formed bonds of cohabitation, of work, of common interests, of affection. The relations between this secular family and the totemic clan are highly complex, as is attested by the diversity of marriage rites. Originally the husband bought a wife from a strange clan, or at least there was an exchange of valuables between one clan and the other, the first handing over one of its members, the second furnishing cattle, fruits, or labour in return. But since the husband assumed responsibility for his wife and her children, he might also receive remuneration from the bride's brothers.

The balance between mystical and economic realities is an unstable one. A man is frequently much more strongly attached to his son than to his nephews; he will prefer to assert himself as father when he is in a position to do so. And this is why every society tends to assume a patriarchal form when man's evolution brings him to the point of self-awareness and the imposition of his will. But it is important to underline the statement that even when he was still perplexed before the mysteries of Life, of Nature, and of Woman, he was never without his power; when, terrified by the dangerous magic of woman, he sets her up as the essential, it is he who poses her as such and thus he really acts as the essential in this voluntary alienation. In spite of the fecund powers that pervade her, man remains woman's master as he is the master of the fertile earth; she is fated to be subjected, owned, exploited like the Nature whose magical fertility she embodies. The prestige she enjoys in men's eyes is bestowed by them; they kneel before the Other, they worship the Goddess Mother. But however puissant she may thus appear, it is only through the conceptions of the male mind that she is apprehended as such.

All the idols made by man, however terrifying they may be, are in point of fact subordinate to him, and that is why he will always have it in his power to destroy them. In primitive societies that subordination is not recognized and openly asserted, but it has immediate existence, in the nature of the case; and it will readily be made use of once man acquires clearer self-consciousness, once he dares to assert himself and offer resistance. And as a matter of fact, even when man felt himself as something given and passive, subject to the accidents of sun and rain, he was also finding fulfilment through transcendence, through project; spirit and will were already asserting themselves against the confusedness and the fortuity of life.

The totemic ancestor, whose multiple incarnations woman assumed, was more or less distinctly a male principle under its animal or arboreal name; woman perpetuated its existence in the flesh, but her role was only nourishing, never creative. In no domain whatever did she create; she maintained the life of the tribe by giving it children and bread, nothing more. She remained doomed to immanence, incarnating only the static aspect of society, closed in upon itself.

97

Whereas man went on monopolizing the functions which threw open that society towards nature and towards the rest of humanity. The only employments worthy of him were war, hunting, fishing; he made conquest of foreign booty and bestowed it on the tribe; war, hunting, and fishing represented an expansion of existence, its projection towards the world. The male remained alone the incarnation of transcendence. He did not as yet have the practical means for wholly dominating Woman-Earth; as yet he did not dare to stand up against her—but already he desired to break away from her.

In my view we must seek in this desire the deep-seated reason for the celebrated custom of exogamy, which is widespread among matrilineal societies. Even if man is ignorant of his part in procreation, marriage is for him a matter of vast importance: through marriage he arrives at the dignity of man's estate, and a plot of land becomes his. He is bound to the clan through his mother, through her to his ancestors and to all that makes up his very substance; but in all his secular functions, in work, in marriage, he aspires to escape from this circle, to assert transcendence over immanence, to open up a future different from the past in which his roots are sunk. The prohibition of incest takes different forms according to the types of relationship recognized in different societies, but from primitive times to our day it keeps the same meaning: what man desires to possess is that which he *is not,* he seeks union with what appears to be *Other* than himself. The wife, therefore, should not share in the mana of the husband, she should be a stranger to him and hence a stranger to his clan. Primitive marriage is sometimes based on an abduction, real or symbolic, and surely violence done upon another is the most obvious affirmation of that one's alterity. In taking his wife by force the warrior demonstrates that he is capable of annexing the wealth of strangers and of bursting the bounds of the destiny assigned to him by birth. Wife-purchase under its various forms—payment of tribute, giving of service—if less dramatic, is of the same import.[1]

[1] We find in the thesis of Lévi-Strauss, already cited, confirmation of this idea, in somewhat different form. It appears from his study that the prohibition of incest is not at all the primal fact underlying exogamy, but rather that it reflects in negative form a positive desire for exogamy. There is no immediate reason why a woman should be unfit for intercourse with the men of her own clan; but it is socially useful for her to be a part of the exchanges through which each clan establishes reciprocal

Little by little man has acted upon his experience, and in his symbolic representations, as in his practical life, it is the male principle that has triumphed. Spirit has prevailed over Life, transcendence over immanence, technique over magic, and reason over superstition. The devaluation of woman represents a necessary stage in the history of humanity, for it is not upon her positive value but upon man's weakness that her prestige is founded. In woman are incarnated the disturbing mysteries of nature, and man escapes her hold when he frees himself from nature. It is the advance from stone to bronze that enables him through his labour to gain mastery of the soil and to master himself. The husbandman is subject to the hazards of the soil, of the germination of seeds, of the seasons ; he is passive, he prays, he waits ; that is why totemic spirits once thronged the world of man ; the peasant is subject to the caprices of these powers round about him. The workman, on the contrary, shapes his tool after his own design ; with his hands he forms it according to his project ; confronting passive nature, he overcomes her resistance and asserts his sovereign will. If he quickens his strokes on the anvil, he finishes his tool sooner, whereas nothing can hasten the ripening of grain. He comes to realize his responsibility for what he is making: his skill or clumsiness will make or break it ; careful, clever, he develops his skill to a point of perfection in which he takes pride: his success depends not upon the favour of the gods but upon himself. He challenges his fellows, he is elated with success. And if he still gives some place to rituals, he feels that exact techniques are much more important ; mystical values rank second and practical interests first. He is not fully liberated from the gods. But he sets them apart from himself as he separates himself from them ; he relegates them to their Olympian

relations with another, instead of keeping to itself. 'Exogamy has a value that is less negative than positive . . . it forbids endogamy . . . not certainly because of any biological danger inherent in consanguineous marriage but because social benefit results from exogamous marriage.' The group should not squander for private purposes the women who constitute one of its possessions, but should use them as a means of communication; if marriage with a woman of the clan is forbidden, 'the only reason is that she is *the same* when she should (and therefore can) become *the other* . . . Women sold into slavery may be the same as those originally offered for exchange in primitive times. All that is required in either case is the *mark of otherness,* which is the result of a certain position in the social structure and not an innate characteristic'.

99

heaven and keeps the terrestrial domain to himself. The great god Pan begins to fade when the first hammer blow resounds and the reign of man begins.

Man learns his power. In the relation of his creative arm to the fabricated object he experiences causation: planted grain may or may not germinate, but metal always reacts in the same way to fire, to tempering, to mechanical treatment. This world of tools could be embraced within clear concepts: rational thought, logic, and mathematics could now appear. The whole concept of the universe is overthrown. The religion of woman was bound to the reign of agriculture, the reign of irreducible duration, of contingency, of chance, of waiting, of mystery; the reign of *Homo faber* is the reign of time manageable as space, of necessary consequences, of the project, of action, of reason. Even when he has to do with the land, he will henceforth have to do with it as workman; he discovers that the soil can be fertilized, that it is good to let it lie fallow, that such and such seeds must be treated in such and such a fashion. It is he who makes the crops grow; he digs canals, he irrigates or drains the land, he lays out roads, he builds temples: he creates a new world.

The peoples who have remained under the thumb of the goddess mother, those who have retained the matrilineal regime, are also those who are arrested at a primitive stage of civilization. Woman was venerated only to the degree that man made himself the slave of his own fears, a party to his own powerlessness: it was in terror and not in love that he worshipped her. He could achieve his destiny only as he began by dethroning her.[1] From then on, it was to be the male principle of creative force, of light, of intelligence, or order, that he would recognize as sovereign. By the side of the goddess mother arises a god, son or lover, who is still subordinate to her but who resembles her trait for trait and is associated with her. He also incarnates a principle of fecundity, appearing as a bull, the Minotaur, the Nile fertilizing the Egyptian lowlands. He dies in autumn and is reborn in the spring, after the wife mother, invulnerable but disconsolate, has devoted her powers to finding his body and bringing

[1] Certainly this condition is necessary, but it is not the whole story: there are patrilineal cultures that have congealed at a primitive stage; others, like that of the Mayas, that have crumbled. There is no absolute superiority or inferiority between societies of maternal or paternal authority, but only the latter have evolved technically and ideologically.

it back to life. We see this couple first appearing in Crete, and we find it again on every Mediterranean shore: in Egypt it is Isis and Horus, Astarte and Adonis in Phoenicia, Cybele and Attis in Asia Minor, and in Hellenic Greece it is Rhea and Zeus.

And then the Great Mother was dethroned. In Egypt, where the situation of woman continues to be exceptionally favourable, Nut, who incarnates the sky, and Isis, the fertile soil, spouse of the Nile, and Osiris remain goddesses of extreme importance; but nevertheless it is Ra, god of the sun, of light, and of virile force, who is supreme. In Babylon Ishtar is no more than wife of Bel-Marduk. He it is who creates all things and assures their harmony. The god of the Semites is male. When Zeus comes to power on high, Gaea, Rhea, and Cybele must abdicate. In Demeter there remains only a divinity of secondary rank, but still imposing. The Vedic gods have spouses, but the latter have no such claim to worship as the former. The Roman Jupiter knows no equal.[1]

Thus the triumph of the patriarchate was neither a matter of chance nor the result of violent revolution. From humanity's beginnings, their biological advantage has enabled the males to affirm their status as sole and sovereign subjects; they have never abdicated this position; they once relinquished a part of their independent existence to Nature and to Woman; but afterwards they won it back. Condemned to play the part of the Other, woman was also condemned to hold only uncertain power: slave or idol, it was never she who chose her lot. 'Men make the gods; women worship them,' as Frazer has said; men indeed decide whether their supreme divinities shall be females or males; woman's place in society is always that which men assign to her; at no time has she ever imposed her own law.

Perhaps, however, if productive work had remained within her strength, woman would have accomplished *with* man the

[1] It is of interest to note (according to BEGOUEN, *Journal de Psychologie*, 1934) that in the Aurignacian period one comes across numerous statuettes of women with sexual features emphasized by exaggeration: they are notable for their plump contours and for the importance given to the vulva. Moreover, one finds in the caves also isolated vulvas, coarsely carved. In the Solutrean and Magdalenian these figures disappear. In the Aurignacian, masculine statuettes are very rare and there are no representations of the male organ. In the Magdalenian one still finds a few vulvas represented and, in contrast, a large number of phalli.

conquest of nature ; the human species would have made its stand against the gods through both males and females ; but woman was unable to avail herself of the promised benefits of the tool. Engels gave only an incomplete explanation for her degradation: it is not enough to say that the invention of bronze and iron profoundly disturbed the equilibrium of the forces of production and that thus the inferior position of woman was brought about ; this inferiority is not sufficient in itself to explain the oppression that woman has suffered. What was unfortunate for her was that while not becoming a fellow workman with the labourer, she was also excluded from the human *Mitsein*. The fact that woman is weak and of inferior productive capacity does not explain this exclusion ; it is because she did not share his way of working and thinking, because she remained in bondage to life's mysterious processes, that the male did not recognize in her a being like himself. Since he did not accept her, since she seemed in his eyes to have the aspect of the *other*, man could not be otherwise than her oppressor. The male will to power and expansion made of woman's incapacity a curse.

Man wished to exhaust the new possibilities opened up by the new techniques: he resorted to a servile labour force, he reduced his fellow man to slavery. The work of the slaves being much more effective than what woman could do, she lost the economic role she had played in the tribe. And in his relation to the slave the master found a much more radical confirmation of his sovereignty than in the limited authority he held over woman. Being venerated and feared because of her fecundity, being *other* than man and sharing the disturbing character of the *other*, woman in a way held man in dependence upon her, while being at the same time dependent upon him ; the reciprocity of the master-slave relation was what she *actually* enjoyed, and through that fact she escaped slavery. But the slave was protected by no taboo, he was nothing but a man in servitude, not different but inferior: the dialectical expression of his relation to his master was to take centuries to come into existence. In organized patriarchal society the slave was only a beast of burden with a human face ; the master exercised tyrannical authority, which exalted his pride—and he turned against woman. Everything he gained he gained against her ; the more powerful he became, the more she declined.

In particular, when he became owner of the land,[1] he

[1] See Part I, chap. III.

claimed also ownership of woman. Formerly he was *possessed* by the mana, by the land; now he *has* a soul, *owns* certain lands; freed from *Woman*, he now demands for himself a woman and a posterity. He wants the work of the family, which he uses to improve his fields, to be totally *his*, and this means that the workers must belong to him: so he enslaves his wife and children. He needs heirs, in whom his earthly life will be prolonged because he hands down his property to them, and who will perform for him after his death the rites and observances needed for the repose of his soul. The cult of domestic gods is superposed upon the organization of private property, and the inheritor fulfils a function at once economic and mystic. Thus from the day when agriculture ceased to be an essentially magic operation and first became creative labour, man realized that he was a generative force; he laid claim to his children and to his crops simultaneously.[1]

In primitive times there was no more important ideological revolution than that which replaced matrilineal with patrilineal descent; thereafter the mother fell to the rank of nurse and servant, while authority and rights belonged to the father, who handed them on to his descendants. Man's necessary part in procreation was realized, but beyond this it was affirmed that only the father engenders, the mother merely nourishes the germ received into her body, as Aeschylus says in the *Eumenides*. Aristotle states that woman is only matter, whereas movement, the male principle, is 'better and more divine'. In making posterity wholly his, man achieved domination of the world and subjugation of woman. Although represented in ancient myths and in Greek drama[2] as the result of violent struggle, in truth the transition to paternal authority was, as we have seen, a matter of gradual change. Man reconquered only what he already possessed, he put the legal

[1] Just as woman was likened to the furrow, so the phallus was to the plough, and vice versa. On a picture of the Kassite epoch representing a plough are traced symbols of the generative act; later the phallus-plough identification was frequently represented in plastic art. The word *Iak* in certain Australasian languages designates both phallus and spade. There is known an Assyrian prayer addressed to a god whose 'plough has fertilized the earth'.

[2] The *Eumenides* represents the triumph of the patriarchate over the matriarchate. The tribunal of the gods declared Orestes to be the son of Agamemnon before he is the son of Clytemnestra—the ancient maternal authority and rights were dead, killed by the audacious revolt of the male!

system into harmony with reality. There was no struggle, no victory, no defeat.

But the old legends have profound meaning. At the moment when man asserts himself as subject and free being, the idea of the Other arises. From that day the relation with the Other is dramatic: the existence of the Other is a threat, a danger. Ancient Greek philosophy showed that alterity, otherness, is the same thing as negation, therefore Evil. To pose the Other is to define a Manichaeism. That is why religions and codes of law treat woman with such hostility as they do. By the time humankind reached the stage of written mythology and law, the patriarchate was definitively established: the males were to write the codes. It was natural for them to give woman a subordinate position, yet one could suppose that they would look upon her with the same benevolence as upon children and cattle—but not at all. While setting up the machinery of woman's oppression, the legislators are afraid of her. Of the ambivalent powers with which she was formerly invested, the evil aspects are now retained: once sacred, she becomes impure. Eve, given to Adam to be his companion, worked the ruin of mankind; when they wish to wreak vengeance upon man, the pagan gods invent woman; and it is the first-born of these female creatures, Pandora, who lets loose all the ills of suffering humanity. The Other—she is passivity confronting activity, diversity that destroys unity, matter as opposed to form, disorder against order. Woman is thus dedicated to Evil. 'There is a good principle, which has created order, light, and man; and a bad principle, which has created chaos, darkness, and woman,' so said Pythagoras. The Laws of Manu define woman as a vile being who should be held in slavery. Leviticus likens her to the beasts of burden owned by the patriarch. The laws of Solon give her no rights. The Roman code puts her under guardianship and asserts her 'imbecility'. Canon law regards her as 'the devil's doorway'. The Koran treats woman with utter scorn.

And yet Evil is necessary to Good, matter to idea, and darkness to light. Man knows that to satisfy his desires, to perpetuate his race, woman is indispensable; he must give her an integral place in society: to the degree in which she accepts the order established by the males, she is freed from her original taint. The idea is very clearly stated in the Laws of Manu: 'a woman assumes through legitimate marriage the very qualities of her husband, like a river that loses itself in the ocean, and she is admitted after death to the same celestial paradise.' And similarly the Bible paints a commendatory portrait of the 'virtuous woman' (Proverbs xxi, 10-31). Christianity respects the consecrated virgin, and the chaste and obedient wife, in spite of its hatred for the flesh. As an associate in the cult, woman can even play an important religious role: the Brahmani in India, the flaminica in Rome, each is as holy as her husband. In the couple the man dominates, but the union of male and female principles remains necessary to the reproductive mechanism, to the maintenance of life, and to the order of society.

It is this ambivalence of the Other, of Woman, that will be reflected in the rest of her history; she will be subjected to man's will up to our own times. But this will is ambiguous: by complete possession and control woman would be abased to the rank of a thing; but man aspires to clothe in his own dignity whatever he conquers and possesses; the Other retains, it seems to him, a little of her primitive magic. How to make of the wife at once a servant and a companion is one of the problems he will seek to solve; his attitude will evolve through the centuries, and that will entail an evolution also in the destiny of woman.[1]

[1] We shall study that evolution in the West. The history of woman in the East, in India, in China, has been in effect that of a long and unchanging slavery. From the Middle Ages to our times, we shall centre this study on France, where the situation is typical.

CHAPTER III

PATRIARCHAL TIMES AND CLASSICAL ANTIQUITY

WOMAN was dethroned by the advent of private property, and her lot through the centuries has been bound up with private property: her history in large part is involved with that of the patrimony. It is easy to grasp the fundamental importance of this institution if one keeps in mind the fact that the owner transfers, alienates, his existence into his property; he cares more for it than for his very life; it overflows the narrow limits of this mortal lifetime, and continues to exist beyond the body's dissolution —the earthly and material incorporation of the immortal soul. But this survival can only come about if the property remains in the hands of its owner: it can be his beyond death only if it belongs to individuals in whom he sees himself projected, who are *his*. To cultivate the paternal domain, to render worship to the manes of the father—these together constitute one and the same obligation for the heir: he assures ancestral survival on earth and in the underworld. Man will not agree, therefore, to share with woman either his gods or his children. He will not succeed in making good his claims wholly and for ever. But at the time of patriarchal power, man wrested from woman all her rights to possess and bequeath property.

For that matter, it seemed logical to do so. When it is admitted that a woman's children are no longer hers, by the same token they have no tie with the group from whence the woman has come. Through marriage woman is now no longer lent from one clan to another: she is torn up by the roots from the group into which she was born, and annexed by her husband's group; he buys her as one buys a farm animal or a slave; he imposes his domestic divinities upon her; and the children born to her belong to the husband's family. If she were an inheritor, she would to an excessive degree transmit the wealth of her father's family to that of her husband; so she is carefully excluded from the succession. But inversely, because she owns nothing, woman does not enjoy the dignity of being a person; she herself forms a part of the patrimony of a man: first of her father, then of her husband. Under the strictly patriarchal regime, the father can, from their birth on, condemn to death both male and female children ; but in the case of the former, society usually limits his power: every normal newborn male is allowed to live, whereas the custom of exposing girl infants is widespread. Among the Arabs there was much infanticide: girls were thrown into ditches as soon as born. It is an act of free generosity on the part of the father to accept the female child ; woman gains entrance into such societies only through a kind of grace bestowed upon her, not legitimately like the male. In any case the defilement of childbirth appears to be much worse for the mother when the baby is a girl: among the Hebrews, Leviticus requires in this case a purification two months longer than when a boy is brought into the world. In societies having the custom of the 'blood price', only a small sum is demanded when the victim is of female sex: her value compared to the male's is like the slave's compared with the free man's.

When she becomes a young girl, the father has all power over her ; when she marries he transfers it *in toto* to the husband. Since a wife is his property like a slave, a beast of burden, or a chattel, a man can naturally have as many wives as he pleases ; polygamy is limited only by economic considerations. The husband can put away his wives at his caprice, society according them almost no security. On the other hand, woman is subjected to a rigorously strict chastity. In spite of taboos, matrilineal societies permit great freedom of behaviour ; prenuptial chastity is rarely required, and adultery is viewed without much severity. On the contrary, when woman becomes man's property, he wants her to be virgin and he requires complete fidelity under threats of extreme penalties. It would be the worst of crimes to risk giving inheritance rights to offspring begotten by some stranger ; hence it is that the paterfamilias has the right to put the guilty spouse to death. As long as private property lasts, so long will marital infidelity on the part of the wife be regarded like the crime of high treason. All codes of law, which to this day have upheld inequality in the matter of adultery, base their argument upon the gravity of the fault of the wife who brings a bastard into the family. And if the right to take the law into his own hands has been abolished since Augustus, the Napoleonic Code still promises the indulgence of the jury to the husband who has himself executed justice.

When the wife belonged at once to the paternal clan and

107

to the conjugal family, she managed to retain a considerable freedom between the two series of bonds, which were confused and even in opposition, each serving to support her against the other: for example, she could often choose her husband according to her fancy, because marriage was only a secular event, not affecting the fundamental structure of society. But in the patriarchal regime she is the property of her father, who marries her off to suit himself. Attached thereafter to her husband's hearth, she is no more than his chattel and the chattel of the clan into which she has been put.

When the family and the private patrimony remain beyond question the bases of society, then woman remains totally submerged. This occurs in the Moslem world. Its structure is feudal; that is, no state has appeared strong enough to unify and rule the different tribes: there is no power to check that of the patriarchal chief. The religion created when the Arab people were warlike and triumphant professed for woman the utmost scorn. The Koran proclaims: 'Men are superior to women on account of the qualities in which God has given them pre-eminence and also because they furnish dowry for women'; woman never had either real power nor mystic prestige. The Bedouin woman works hard, she ploughs and carries burdens: thus she sets up with her spouse a bond of reciprocal dependence; she walks abroad freely with uncovered face. The veiled and sequestered Moslem woman is still today in most social strata a kind of slave.

I recall seeing in a primitive village of Tunisia a subterranean cavern in which four women were squatting: the old one-eyed and toothless wife, her face horribly devastated, was cooking dough on a small brazier in the midst of an acrid smoke; two wives somewhat younger, but almost as disfigured, were lulling children in their arms—one was giving suck; seated before a loom, a young idol magnificently decked out in silk, gold, and silver was knotting threads of wool. As I left this gloomy cave—kingdom of immanence, womb, and tomb—in the corridor leading upwards towards the light of day I passed the male, dressed in white, well groomed, smiling, sunny. He was returning from the marketplace, where he had discussed world affairs with other men; he would pass some hours in this retreat of his at the heart of the vast universe to which he belonged, from which he was not separated. For the withered old women, for the young wife doomed to the same rapid decay, there was no universe other than the smoky cave, whence they emerged only at night, silent and veiled.

The Jews of Biblical times had much the same customs as the Arabs. The patriarchs were polygamous, and they could put away their wives almost at will; it was required under severe penalties that the young wife be turned over to her husband a virgin; in case of adultery, the wife was stoned; she was kept in the confinement of domestic duties, as the Biblical portrait of the virtuous woman proves: 'She seeketh wool, and flax . . . she riseth also while it is yet night . . . her candle goeth not out by night . . . she eateth not the bread of idleness.' Though chaste and industrious, she is ceremonially unclean, surrounded with taboos; her testimony is not acceptable in court. Ecclesiastes speaks of her with the most profound disgust: 'And I find more bitter than death the woman, whose heart is snares and nets, and her hands as bands . . . one man among a thousand have I found; but a woman among all those have I not found.' Custom, if not the law, required that at the death of her husband the widow should marry a brother of the departed.

This custom, called the *levirate,* is found among many Oriental peoples. In all regimes where woman is under guardianship, one of the problems that must be faced is what to do with widows. The most extreme solution is to sacrifice them on the tomb of the husband. But it is not true that even in India the law has ever required such holocausts; the Laws of Manu permit wife to survive husband. The spectacular suicides were never more than an aristocratic fashion. Much more frequently the widow is handed over to the heirs of the husband. The levirate sometimes takes the form of polyandry; to forestall the uncertainties of widowhood, all the brothers in a family are given as husbands to one woman, a custom that serves also to protect the tribe against the possible infertility of the husband. According to a passage in Caesar, it appears that in Brittany all the men of a family had thus in common a certain number of women.

The patriarchate was not established everywhere in this radical form. In Babylon the laws of Hammurabi acknowledged certain rights of woman; she receives a part of the paternal estate, and when she marries, her father provides a dowry. In Persia polygamy was customary; the wife was required to be absolutely obedient to her husband, chosen for her by her father when she was of marriageable age; but she was held in honour more than among most Oriental peoples. Incest was not forbidden, and marriage was frequent between brother and sister. The wife was responsible for the education of children—boys up to the age of seven and girls up to marriage. She could receive a part of her husband's estate if the son showed himself unworthy ; if she was a 'privileged spouse' she was entrusted with the guardianship of minor children and the management of business matters if the husband died without having an adult son. The marriage regulations show clearly the importance that the existence of a posterity had for the head of a family. It appears that there were five forms of marriage: [1] (1) When the woman married with her parents' consent, she was called a 'privileged spouse' ; her children belonged to her husband. (2) When a woman was an only child, the first of her children was sent back to her parents to take the place of their daughter ; after this the wife became a 'privileged spouse'. (3) If a man died unmarried, his family dowered and received in marriage some woman from outside, called an adopted wife ; half of her children belonged to the deceased, the other half to her living husband. (4) A widow without children when remarried was called a servant wife ; she was bound to assign half of the children of her second marriage to the dead husband. (5) The woman who married without the consent of her parents could not inherit from them before her oldest son, become of age, had given her as 'privileged spouse' to his own father ; if her husband died before this, she was regarded as a minor and put under guardianship. The institution of the adopted wife and the servant wife enabled every man to be survived by descendants, to whom he was not necessarily connected by a blood relationship. This confirms what I was saying above ; for this relationship was in a way invented by man in the wish to acquire beyond his own death an immortality on earth and in the underworld.

It was in Egypt that woman enjoyed most favourable conditions. The goddess mothers retained their prestige in becoming wives ; the couple was the religious and social unit ; woman seemed to be allied with and complementary to man. Her magic was so slightly hostile that even the fear of incest was overcome and sister and wife were combined without hesitation. [2] Woman had the same rights as man, the same

[1] This outline follows C. HUART, *Perse antique et la civilisation iranienne*, pp. 195-6.
[2] In certain cases, at least, the brother was bound to marry his sister.

powers in court; she inherited, she owned property. This remarkably fortunate situation was by no means due to chance: it came from the fact that in ancient Egypt the land belonged to the king and to the higher castes of priests and soldiers; private individuals could have only the use and produce of landed property—the usufruct—the land itself remained inalienable. Inherited property had little value, and apportioning it caused no difficulty. Because of the absence of private patrimony, woman retained the dignity of a person. She married without compulsion and if widowed she could remarry at her pleasure. The male practised polygamy; but though all the children were legitimate, there was only one real wife, the one who alone was associated in religion and bound to him legally; the others were only slaves without any rights at all. The chief wife did not change status in marrying: she remained mistress of her property and free to do business. When Pharaoh Bochoris established private property, woman occupied so strong a position that she could not be dislodged; Bochoris opened the era of contracts, and marriage itself became contractual.

There were three types of marriage contracts: one concerned servile marriage; the woman became the man's property, but there was sometimes the specification that he would have no other concubine; at the same time the legitimate spouse was regarded as the man's equal, and all their goods were held in common; often the husband agreed to pay her a sum of money in case of divorce. This custom led later to a type of contract particularly favourable to the wife: the husband granted to her an artificial trust. There were severe penalties against adultery, but divorce was almost free for both parties. The putting into effect of these contracts tended strongly to reduce polygamy; the women monopolized the fortunes and bequeathed them to their children, leading to the advent of a plutocratic class. Ptolemy Philopater decreed that women could no longer dispose of their property without authorization by their husbands, which made them permanent minors. But even at the time when they had a privileged status, unique in the ancient world, women were not socially the equals of men. Sharing in religion and in government, they could act as regent, but the pharaoh was male; the priests and soldiers were men; women took only a secondary part in public life; and in private life there was demanded of them a fidelity without reciprocity.

The customs of the Greeks remained very similar to the

Oriental; but they did not include polygamy. Just why is unknown. It is true that maintenance of a harem has always been a heavy expense: it was Solomon in all his glory, the sultans of *The Arabian Nights,* kings, chieftains, the rich, who could indulge themselves in the luxury of a vast seraglio; the average man was content with three or four wives; the peasant rarely had more than two. Besides—except in Egypt, where there was no special private property—regard for preserving the patrimony intact led to the bestowal on the eldest son of special rights in the paternal estate. On this account there was established a hierarchy among the wives, the mother of the chief heir being clothed in a dignity far above that of the others. If the wife had property of her own, if she had a dowry, she was for her husband a person: he was joined to her by a bond at once religious and exclusive.

On the basis of this situation, no doubt, was established the custom of recognizing only a single wife. But in point of fact the Greek citizen remained agreeably polygamous in practice, since he could satisfy his desires with the prostitutes of the city and the handmaidens of his gynaeceum. 'We have hetairas for the pleasures of the spirit,' said Demosthenes, *'pallages* (concubines) for sensual pleasure, and wives to give us sons.' The concubine replaced the wife in the master's bed when she was ill, indisposed, pregnant, or recovering from childbirth; thus there is no great difference between gynaeceum and harem. In Athens the wife was shut up in her quarters, held under severe constraint by law, and watched over by special magistrates. She remained all her life a perpetual minor, under the control of her guardian, who might be her father, her husband, the latter's heir, or, in default of these, the State, represented by public officials. These were her masters, and she was at their disposal like a commodity, the control of the guardian extending over both her person and her property. The guardian could transfer his rights at will: the father gave his daughter in marriage or into adoption; the husband could put away his wife and hand her over to a new husband. Greek law, however, assured to the wife a dowry, which was used for her maintenance and was to be restored in full if the marriage was dissolved; the law also authorized the wife in certain rare cases to ask for divorce; but these were the only guarantees granted her by society. The whole estate was, of course, bequeathed to male children, the dowry representing, not property acquired

112

through relationship, but a kind of contribution required of the guardian. Yet, thanks to the custom of the dowry, the widow no longer passed like a hereditary possession into the hands of her husband's heirs: she was restored to the guardianship of her parents.

One of the problems arising in societies based on inheritance through the male line is what happens to the estate if there are no male descendants. The Greeks established the custom of the *epiclerate*: the female heir must marry her eldest relative in her father's family (genos); thus the property left to her by her father would be passed on to children belonging to the same group, the domain would remain the property of the family (genos). The *epiclere* was not a female heir—merely a means for producing a male heir. This custom put her wholly at man's mercy, since she was turned over automatically to the first-born of the males of her family, who most often turned out to be an old man.

Since the oppression of woman has its cause in the will to perpetuate the family and to keep the patrimony intact, woman escapes complete dependency to the degree in which she escapes from the family; if a society that forbids private property also rejects the family, the lot of woman in it is found to be considerably ameliorated. In Sparta the communal regime was in force, and it was the only Greek city in which woman was treated almost on an equality with man. The girls were brought up like the boys; the wife was not confined in her husband's domicile: indeed, he was allowed to visit her only furtively, by night; and his wife was so little his property that on eugenic grounds another man could demand union with her. The very idea of adultery disappeared when the patrimony disappeared; all children belonged in common to the city as a whole, and women were no longer jealously enslaved to one master; or, inversely, one may say that the citizen, possessing neither private wealth nor specific ancestry, was no longer in possession of woman. Women underwent the servitude of maternity as did men the servitude of war; but beyond the fulfilling of this civic duty, no restraint was put upon their liberty.

Along with the free women just commented on and the slaves living within the genos, there were also prostitutes in Greece. Primitive peoples practised the prostitution of hospitality—a yielding up of woman to the transient guest, which doubtless had its mystic justification—and also sacred prosti-

113

tution, intended to release for the common good the mysterious powers of fecundation. These customs existed in classical antiquity. Herodotus relates that in the fifth century B.C. each Babylonian woman was in duty bound once in her lifetime to yield herself to a stranger in the temple of Mylitta for money, which she contributed to the wealth of the temple; thereafter she went home to lead a chaste life. Religious prostitution has persisted to the present time among the dancing girls of Egypt and the bayaderes of India, who constitute respected castes of musicians and dancers. But usually, in Egypt, in India, in western Asia, sacred prostitution passed over into legal, mercenary prostitution, the sacerdotal class finding this traffic profitable. Even among the Hebrews there were mercenary prostitutes.

In Greece, especially along the seacoast, in the islands, and in the cities thronged with visitors, were the temples in which were to be found the 'young girls hospitable to strangers', as Pindar called them. The money they earned was destined for the religious establishment—that is, for the priests and indirectly for their maintenance. In reality, there was hypocritical exploitation—at Corinth and elsewhere—of the sexual needs of sailors and travellers, and it was already venal or mercenary prostitution in essence. It remained for Solon to make an institution of the traffic. He bought Asiatic slaves and shut them up in the 'dicterions' located near the temple of Venus at Athens, not far from the port. The management was in the hands of *pornotropoi*, who were responsible for the financial administration of the establishment. Each girl received wages, and the net profit went to the State. Afterwards private establishments, *kapaileia*, were opened, with a red priapus serving as business sign. Before long, in addition to the slaves, Greek women of low degree were taken in as boarders. The 'dicterions' were regarded as so essential that they received recognition as inviolable places of refuge. The prostitutes were persons of low repute, however; they had no social rights, their children were excused from supporting them, they had to wear a special costume of many-coloured cloth, ornamented with bouquets, and they had to dye their hair with saffron.

In addition to the women of the 'dicterions', there were also free courtesans, who can be placed in three categories: the dicteriads, much like the licensed prostitutes of today; the auletrids, dancers and flute-players; and the hetairas, women of the demi-monde, mostly from Corinth, who car-

114

ried on recognized liaisons with the most notable men of Greece and who played the social role of the modern 'woman of the world'. The first were recruited among freed women and Greek girls of the lower classes; they were exploited by the procurers and led a life of misery. The second were often able to get rich because of their talent as musicians; most celebrated was Lamia, mistress of an Egyptian Ptolemy, and then of his conqueror, Demetrius Poliorcetes, King of Macedonia. As for the third and last category, it is well known that several shared the glory of their lovers. Free to make disposal of themselves and of their fortunes, intelligent, cultivated, artistic, they were treated as persons by the men who found enchantment in their company. By virtue of the fact that they escaped from the family and lived on the fringes of society, they escaped also from man; they could therefore seem to him to be fellow beings, almost equals. In Aspasia, in Phryne, in Lais was made manifest the superiority of the free woman over the respectable mother of a family.

These brilliant exceptions apart, woman in Greece was reduced to semi-slavery, without even the liberty to complain. In the great classical period woman was firmly shut away in the gynaeceum; Pericles said that 'the best woman is she of whom men speak the least'. Plato aroused the raillery of Aristophanes when he advocated the admission of matrons to the administration of the Republic and proposed giving girls a liberal education. But according to Xenophon, wife and husband were strangers, and in general the wife was required to be a watchful mistress of the house, prudent, economical, industrious as a bee, a model stewardess. In spite of this modest status of woman, the Greeks were profoundly misogynous. From ancient epigrammatists to the classical writers, woman was constantly under attack, not for loose conduct—she was too severely controlled for that—and not because she represented the flesh; it was especially the burdens and discomforts of marriage that weighed on the men. We must suppose that in spite of woman's low condition she none the less held a place of importance in the house; she might sometimes disobey, and she could overwhelm her husband with scenes, tears, and nagging, so that marriage, intended to enslave woman, was also a ball and chain for man. In the figure of Xantippe are summed up all the grievances of the Greek citizen against the shrewish wife and against the adversities of married life.

In Rome it was the conflict between family and State that determined the history of woman. Etruscan society was matrilineal, and it is probable that in the time of the monarchy Rome still practised exogamy under a matrilineal regime: the Latin kings did not hand on power from one to another in the hereditary fashion. It is certainly true after the death of Tarquin patriarchal authority was established: agricultural property, the private estate—therefore the family—became the unitary basis of society. Woman was to be closely bound to the patrimony and hence to the family group. The laws even deprived her of the protection extended to Greek women; she lives a life of legal incapacity and of servitude. She was, of course, excluded from public affairs, all 'masculine' positions being severely forbidden to her; and in her civil life she was a permanent minor. She was not directly deprived of her share in the paternal heritage, but by indirect means she was prevented from exercising control of it—she was put under the authority of a guardian. 'Guardianship,' says Gaius, 'was established in the interest of the guardians themselves, so that the woman, whose presumptive heirs they are, could not rob them of the heritage by willing it to others, nor reduce it by expenditures and debts.'

The first guardian of a woman was her father; in his absence his male relatives performed this function. When a woman married, she passed into the hands of her husband; there were three types of marriage: the *conferatio*, in which the couple offered to the capitoline Jupiter a cake of wheat in the presence of the *flamen dialis*; the *coemptio*, a fictitious sale in which the plebeian father 'mancipated' his daughter to the husband; and the *usus*, the result of a year's cohabitation. All these were with '*manu*', meaning that the husband replaced the father or other guardian; his wife became like one of his daughters, and he had complete control henceforth over her person and her property. But from the time of the law of the Twelve Tables, because the Roman woman belonged at once to the paternal and the conjugal clans, conflicts arose, which were at the source of her legal emancipation. In fact, marriage with *manu* despoiled the agnate guardians. To protect these paternal relatives, a form of marriage *sine manu* came in; here the woman's property remained under the guardian's control, the husband acquired rights over her person only. Even this power was shared with her paterfamilias, who retained an absolute authority over his daughter. The domestic tribunal was empowered to settle the disputes

116

that could bring father and husband into conflict; such a court permitted the wife an appeal from father to husband or from husband to father; she was not the chattel of any one individual. Moreover, although the family was very powerful (as is proved by the very existence of this tribunal, independent of the public tribunals), the father and head of a family was before all a citizen. His authority was unlimited, he was absolute ruler of wife and children; but these were not his property; rather, he controlled their existence for the public good: the wife who brought children into the world and whose domestic labour often included farm work was most useful to the country and was profoundly respected.

We observe here a very important fact that we shall come upon throughout the course of history: abstract rights are not enough to define the actual concrete situation of woman; this depends in large part on her economic role; and frequently abstract liberty and concrete powers vary in inverse ratio. Legally more enslaved than the Greek, the woman of Rome was in practice much more deeply integrated in society. At home she sat in the atrium, the centre of the dwelling, instead of being hidden away in the gynaeceum; she directed the work of the slaves; she guided the education of the children, and frequently she influenced them up to a considerable age. She shared the labours and cares of her husband, she was regarded as co-owner of his property. The matron was called *domina*; she was mistress of the home, associate in religion—not the slave, but the companion of man. The tie that bound her to him was so sacred that in five centuries there was not a single divorce. Women were not restricted to their quarters, being present at meals and celebrations and going to the theatre. In the street men gave them right of way, consuls and lictors made room for them to pass. Woman played a prominent role in history, according to such legends as those of the Sabine women, Lucretia, and Virginia; Coriolanus yielded to the supplications of his mother and his wife; the law of Lucinius, sanctioning the triumph of Roman democracy, was inspired by his wife; Cornelia forged the souls of the Gracchi. 'Everywhere men rule over women,' said Cato, 'and we who govern all men are ourselves governed by our women.'

Little by little the legal status of the Rome woman was brought into agreement with her actual condition. At the time of the patrician oligarchy each head of a family was an independent sovereign within the Republic; but when the power

117

of the State became firmly established, it opposed the concentration of wealth and the arrogance of the powerful families. The domestic tribunal disappeared before the public courts. And woman gained increasingly important rights. Four authorities had at first limited her freedom: the father and husband had control of her person, the guardian and the *manus* of her property. The State took advantage of the opposition of the father and husband in order to limit their rights: cases of adultery, divorce, and so on were to be judged in the State courts. Similarly, *manus* and guardianship were destroyed, the one by the other. For the guardian's benefit the *manus* had already been separated from marriage; later the *manus* became an expedient used by women in escaping their guardians, whether by contracting fictitious marriages or by securing complaisant guardians from the father or the State. Under the legislation of the Empire, guardianship was to be entirely abolished.

Woman also gained a positive guarantee of independence: her father was required to provide her with a dowry. This did not go back to her male relatives after dissolution of the marriage, and it never belonged to her husband; the wife could at any time demand its restitution through immediate divorce, which put the man at her mercy. According to Plautus, 'In accepting the dowry, he sold his power.' From the end of the Republic on, the mother was entitled to the respect of her children on an equality with the father; she was entrusted with the care of her offspring in case of guardianship or of bad conduct on the part of her husband. Under Hadrian, an act of the Senate conferred upon her—when she had three children and when any of them died without issue—the right to inherit from each of them intestate. And under Marcus Aurelius the evolution of the Roman family was completed: from the year 178 on, children were the heirs of their mother, triumphing over the male relatives; henceforth the family was based upon *conjunctio sanguinis* and the mother took a place of equality with the father; the daughter inherited like her brothers.

We observe in the history of Roman law, however, a tendency contradicting that which I have just described; the power of the State, while making woman independent of the family, took her back under its own guardianship; it made her legally incompetent in various ways.

Indeed, she would take on a disturbing importance if she could be at once wealthy and independent; so it was going to be necessary to take away from her with one hand what had been yielded to her with the other. The Oppian law, forbidding luxury to Roman women, was passed at the moment when Hannibal was threatening Rome; once the danger was past, the women demanded that it be repealed. In an oration, Cato demanded its retention; but the appearance of the matrons assembled in the public square carried the day against him. Various laws, increasing in severity as the mores became more loose, were later proposed, but without much success: they hardly did more than give rise to fraud. Only the Velleian act of the Senate triumphed, forbidding women to 'intercede' for others—that is, to enter into contracts with others—which deprived her of almost every legal capacity. Thus it was just when woman was most fully emancipated that the inferiority of her sex was asserted, affording a remarkable example of the process of male justification of which I have spoken: when women's rights as daughter, wife, or sister are no longer limited, it is her equality with man, as a sex, that is denied her; 'the imbecility, the weakness of the sex' is alleged, in domineering fashion.

The fact is that the matrons made no very good use of their new liberty; but it is also true that they were not allowed to turn it to positive account. The result of these two contrary tendencies—an individualist tendency that freed woman from the family and a statist tendency that infringed upon her as an individual—was to make her situation unbalanced. She could inherit, she has equal rights with the father in regard to the children, she could testify. Thanks to the institution of the dowry, she escaped conjugal oppression, she could divorce and remarry at will; but she was emancipated only in a negative way, since she was offered no concrete employment of her powers. Economic freedom remained abstract, since it produced no political power. Thus it was that, lacking equal capacity to *act*, the Roman women *demonstrated*: they swarmed tumultuously through the city, they besieged the courts, they fomented plots, they raised objections, stirred up civil strife; in procession they sought out the statue of the Mother of Gods and bore it along the Tiber, thus introducing Oriental divinities into Rome; in the year 114 the scandal of the Vestal Virgins burst forth and their organization was suppressed.

When the collapse of the family made the ancient virtues of private life useless and outdated, there was no longer any established morality for woman, since public life and its virtues remained inaccessible to her. Women could choose between two solutions: either continue obstinately to respect the values of their grandmothers, or no longer recognize any values. At the end of the first century and the beginning of the second we see many women continuing to be the companions and associates of their husbands as they were during the Republic: Plotina shared the glory and the responsibilities of Trajan; Sabina made herself so famous through her benefactions that in her lifetime she was deified in statuary; under Tiberius, Sextia refused to survive Aemilius Scaurrus, and Pascea to survive Pomponius Labeus; Pauline opened her veins with Seneca; Pliny the Younger had made famous Arria's *'non dolet, Paete'*;[1] Martial praised Claudia Rufina, Virginia, and Sulpicia as wives beyond reproach and devoted mothers. But there were many women who refused maternity and who helped to raise the divorce rate. The laws still forbade adultery, so some matrons went so far as to have themselves registered as prostitutes in order to facilitate their debauchery.[2]

Up to that time Latin literature had always treated women respectfully, but then the satirists were let loose against them. They attacked no woman in general but specifically women of that particular time. Juvenal reproached them for their lewdness and gluttony; he found fault with them for aspiring to men's occupations—they meddled in politics, plunged into the files of legal papers, disputed with grammarians and rhetoricians, went in passionately for hunting, chariot racing, fencing, and wrestling. They were rivals of the men, especially in their taste for amusement and in their vices; they lacked sufficient education to envisage higher aims; and besides, no goal was set up for them; action was still forbidden for them. The Roman woman of the old Republic had a place on earth, but she was chained to it for lack of abstract rights and economic independence; the Roman woman of the decline was the typical product of false emancipation, having only an empty liberty in a world of which man remained in fact the sole master: she was free—but for nothing.

[1] When her husband, Paetus, was in serious trouble with the authorities, Arria stabbed herself, saying: 'It does not hurt, Paetus,' which encouraged him to do likewise.—Tr.
[2] Rome, like Greece, officially tolerated prostitution. There were two classes of courtesans: those who were confined in brothels, and the 'good prostitutes', those who practised their profession in freedom but were not allowed to wear the usual married woman's costume. They had some influence on fashion, dress, and the arts, but they never occupied any such lofty position as the Athenian hetairas.

CHAPTER IV

THROUGH THE MIDDLE AGES TO
EIGHTEENTH-CENTURY FRANCE

T H E evolution of woman's condition was not a con-
tinuous process. When the great invasions came, all
civilization was again called in question. Roman law
itself came under the influence of a new ideology, Christianity ; and in the following centuries the barbarians succeeded
in imposing their laws. The economic, social, and political
situation was turned upside down: that of woman felt the
repercussion.

Christian ideology has contributed no little to the oppression of woman. Doubtless there is in the Gospel a breath of
charity that extends to women as to lepers ; and it was, to be
sure, humble folk, slaves, and women who clung most passionately to the new law. In early Christian times women were
treated with relative honour when they submitted themselves
to the yoke of the Church ; they bore witness as martyrs side
by side with men. But they could take only a secondary place
as participants in worship, the 'deaconesses' were authorized
to carry out only such lay tasks as caring for the sick and
aiding the poor. And if marriage was to be held to be an institution demanding mutual fidelity, it seemed obvious that
the wife should be totally subordinated to her husband:
through St. Paul the Jewish tradition, savagely anti-feminist,
was affirmed.

St. Paul enjoined self-effacement and discretion upon
women ; he based the subordination of woman to man upon
both the Old and the New Testaments. 'For the man is not
of the woman ; but the woman of the man. Neither was the
man created for the woman ; but the woman for the man.'
And in another place: 'For the husband is the head of the
wife, even as Christ is the head of the church . . . Therefore as the church is subject unto Christ, so let the wives be
to their own husbands in everything.' In a religion that holds
the flesh accursed, woman becomes the devil's most fearsome
temptation. Tertullian writes: 'Woman, you are the devil's

doorway. You have led astray one whom the devil would not dare attack directly. It is your fault that the Son of God had to die; you should always go in mourning and in rags.' St. Ambrose: 'Adam was led to sin by Eve and not Eve by Adam. It is just and right that woman accept as lord and master him whom she led to sin.' And St. John Chrysostom: 'Among all savage beasts none is found so harmful as woman."' When the canon law was set up in the fourth century, marriage was viewed as a concession to human frailty, something incompatible with Christian perfection. 'Let us take axe in hand and cut off at its roots the fruitless tree of marriage,' wrote St. Jerome. From the time of Gregory VI, when celibacy was imposed on the priesthood, the dangerous character of woman was more severely emphasized: all the Fathers of the Church proclaimed her abjectly evil nature. St. Thomas was true to this tradition when he declared that woman is only an 'occasional' and incomplete being, a kind of imperfect man. 'Man is above woman, as Christ is above man,' he writes. 'It is unchangeable that woman is destined to live under man's influence, and has no authority from her lord.' Moreover, the canon law admitted no other matrimonial regime than the dowry scheme, which made woman legally incompetent and powerless. Not only did the masculine occupations remain closed to her, but she was forbidden to make depositions in court, and her testimony was not recognized as having weight. The emperors were affected to some extent by the influence of the Church Fathers. Justinian's legislation honoured woman as wife and mother, but held her subservient to these functions; it was not to her sex but to her situation within the family that she owed her legal incompetence. Divorce was forbidden and marriage was required to be performed in public. The mother's authority over her children was equal to the father's, and she had the same rights in their inheritances; if her husband died she became their legal guardian. The Velleian act of the Senate was modified so that in future a woman could make contracts for the benefit of a third party; but she could not contract for her husband; her dowry became inalienable—it was the patrimony of the children and she was forbidden to dispose of it.

These laws came into contact with Germanic traditions in the territories occupied by the barbarians. In peacetime the Germans had no chieftain, the family being an independent society in which woman was completely under male domination, though she was respected and had some rights. Marriage was monogamous, and adultery was severely punished. In wartime the wife followed her husband into battle, sharing his lot in life and death, as Tacitus reports. Woman's inferiority was due to physical weakness and was not moral, and since woman could act as priestesses and prophetesses, they may have been better educated than the men.

These traditions were continued into the Middle Ages, woman being in a state of absolute dependence on father and husband. The Franks did not maintain the Germanic chastity: polgamy was practised ; woman was married without her consent, and put away at her husband's caprice ; and she was treated as a servant. The laws gave her strong protection from injury and insult, but only as man's property and mother of his children. As the State became powerful, the same changes occurred as in Rome: guardianship became a public charge, protecting woman, but also continuing her enslavement.

When feudalism emerged from the convulsions of the early Middle Ages, woman's position seems to have been most uncertain. Feudalism involved confusion of authority between sovereignty and property, between public and private rights and powers. This explains why woman was alternately elevated and abased under this regime. At first she had no private rights because she had no political power, and this was because the social order up to the eleventh century was founded on might alone, and the fief was property held by military force, a power not wielded by woman. Later, woman could inherit in the absence of male heirs ; but her husband was guardian and exercised control over the fief and its income ; she was a part of the fief, by no means emancipated.

The domain was no longer a family affair, as in the time of the Roman gens: it belonged to the suzerain ; and woman also. He chose her husband, and her children belonged to him rather than to her husband, being destined to become vassals who would protect his wealth. Thus she was slave of the domain and of the master of this domain through the 'protection' of a husband imposed upon her: there have been few periods in which her lot was harder. An heiress—that meant land and a castle. At twelve or less she might be given in marriage to some baron. But more marriages meant more property, so annulments were frequent, hypocritically authorized by the Church. Pretexts were easily found in the rules against marriage between persons related in even remote degree and not necessarily by blood. Many women of the eleventh century had been thus repudiated four or five times.

If widowed, woman was expected to accept at once a new master. In the *chansons de geste* we see Charlemagne marrying in a group all the widows of his barons killed in Spain ; and many epic poems tell of king or baron disposing tyrannically of girls and widows. Wives were beaten, chastised, dragged by the hair. The knight was not interested in women ; his horse seemed much more valuable to him. In the *chansons de geste* young women always made the advances, but once they were married, a one-sided fidelity was demanded of them. Girls were brought up rudely, with rough physical exercises and without modesty or much education. When grown up, they hunted wild beasts, made difficult pilgrimages, defended the fief when the master was abroad. Some of these chatelaines were avaricious, perfidious, cruel, tyrannical, like the men ; grim tales of their violence have come down to us. But all such were exceptions ; ordinarily the chatelaine passed her days in spinning, saying her prayers, waiting on her husband, and dying of boredom.

The 'knightly love' appearing in the Midi in the twelfth century may have softened woman's lot a little, whether it arose from the relations between the lady and her young vassals or from the cult of the Virgin or from the love of God in general. There is doubt that the courts of love ever really existed, but it is sure that the Church exalted the cult of the mother of the Redeemer to such a degree that we can say that in the thirteenth century God had been made woman. And the life of ease of noble dames permitted conversation, polite manners, and poetry to flourish. Learned women, such as Eleanor of Aquitaine and Blanche of Navarre, supported poets, and a widespread cultural flowering lent to woman a new prestige. Knightly love has often been regarded as platonic ; but the truth is that the feudal husband was guardian and tyrant, and the wife sought an extra-marital lover ; knightly love was a compensation for the barbarism of the official mores. As Engels remarks : 'Love, in the modern sense of the word, appeared in antiquity only outside the bounds of official society. The point where antiquity stopped in its search for sexual love is just where the Middle Ages started : adultery.' And that is indeed the form that love will assume as long as the institution of marriage lasts.

But it was not knightly love nor was it religion but quite other causes that enabled woman to gain some ground as feudalism came to an end. As royal power increased, the feudal lord gradually lost much of his authority, including that of deciding vassal marriages, and the right to use the wealth of his wards. When the fief contributed money instead of military service to the crown, it became a mere patrimony and there was no longer any reason why the two sexes should not be treated on a footing of equality. In France the unmarried or widowed woman had all the rights of man; as proprietor of a fief, she administered justice, signed treaties, decreed laws. She even played a military role, commanding troops and joining combat: there were female soldiers before Joan of Arc, and if the Maid caused astonishment, she did not scandalize.

So many factors combine against women's independence, however, that they never seem to have been all abolished at once. Physical weakness no longer counted, but in the case of married women subordination remained useful to society. Hence marital authority survived the passing of feudalism. We see the same paradox that exists today: the woman who is most fully integrated in society has the fewest privileges. Under civil feudalism marriage remained as it was under military feudalism: the husband was still his wife's guardian. When the bourgeoisie arose, it followed the same laws; the girl and the widow have the rights of man; but in marriage woman was a ward, to be beaten, her conduct watched over in detail, and her fortune used at will. The interests of property require among nobility and bourgeoisie that a single administrator take charge. This could be a single woman; her abilities were admitted; but from feudal times to our days the married woman has been deliberately sacrificed to private property. The richer the husband, the greater the dependence of the wife; the more powerful he feels socially and economically, the more authoritatively he plays the paterfamilias. On the contrary, a common poverty makes the conjugal tie a reciprocal tie. Neither feudalism nor the Church freed woman. It was rather in emerging from serfdom that the passage from the patriarchal to the truly conjugal family was accomplished. The serf and his wife owned nothing; they had the use of house and furnishings, but that was no reason for the man to try to be master of a wife without wealth. On the contrary, common interests brought them together and raised the wife to the rank of companion. When serfdom was abolished, poverty remained; husband and wife lived on a footing of equality in small rural communities and among the workers; in free labour woman found real autonomy because she played an economic and social part of real importance. In the comedies and fables of the Middle Ages is reflected a society of workers, small merchants, and peasants in which the husband had no advantages over his wife except the strength to beat her ; but she opposed guile to force, and the pair thus lived in equality. Meanwhile the rich woman paid with her subjection for her idleness.

Woman still retained a few privileges in the Middle Ages, but in the sixteenth century were codified the laws that lasted all through the Old Regime ; the feudal mores were gone and nothing protected woman from man's wish to chain her to the hearth. The code denied woman access to 'masculine' positions, deprived her of all civil capacities, kept her, while unmarried, under the guardianship of her father, who sent her into a convent if she failed to marry later, and if she did marry put her and her property and children completely under her husband's authority. He was held responsible for her debts and conduct, and she had little direct relation with public authorities or persons who were strangers to her family. She seemed in work and in motherhood more a servant than an associate: the objects, the values, the beings she created were not her own wealth but belonged to the family, therefore to the man who was its head. In other countries woman was no better off ; her political rights were none and the mores were severe. All the European legal codes were erected on a basis of canon law, Roman law, and Germanic law—all unfavourable to woman. Every country had private property and the family and was regulated according to the demands of these institutions.

In all these countries one of the results of the 'honest woman's' enslavement to the family was the existence of prostitution. Maintained hypocritically on the fringes of society, the prostitutes played a most important part in it. Christianity poured out its scorn upon them, but accepted them as a necessary evil. Both St. Augustine and St. Thomas asserted that the suppression of prostitution would mean the disruption of society by debauch: 'Prostitutes are to a city what sewers are to a palace.' In the early Middle Ages the mores were so licentious that whores were hardly needed ; but when the bourgeois family was established and rigorous monogamy became the rule, a man had to look for pleasure outside the home.

Against prostitution the efforts of Charlemagne, and later those of Charles IX in France, and those of Maria Theresa

in Austria in the eighteenth century[1] were all alike failures.
The organization of society made prostitution necessary. As
Schopenhauer was to put it pompously: 'Prostitutes are
human sacrifices on the altar of monogamy.' Lecky, historian
of European morals, formulated the same idea somewhat
differently: 'Supreme type of vice, they are the greatest guardians of virtue.' The usury of the Jews and the extra-conju-
gal sexuality of the prostitutes were alike denounced by
Church and State; but society could not get along without
financial speculation and extra-marital love; these functions
were therefore assigned to wretched castes, segregated in
ghettoes or in restricted quarters. The prostitutes like the Jews
were obliged to wear distinctive signs on their clothing; they
were helpless against the police; for most, life was difficult.
But many prostitutes were free; some made a good living.
As in the time of the Greek hetairas, the high life of gallantry
offered more opportunities to feminine individualism than did
the life of the 'honest woman'.

In France the single woman occupied a peculiar position;
her independence was in startling contrast to the bondage of
the wife; she was a remarkable personage. But then the mores
deprived her of all that the law had bestowed; she possessed
civil rights—but these were abstract and empty; she enjoyed
neither economic autonomy nor social dignity; generally the
old maid spent her life in the shadow of her father's family
or joined others like her within the convents, where she
scarcely knew any other form of liberty than disobedience
and sin—just as the Roman women of the decadence found
freedom only through vice. Negation was still the lot of
women, since their emancipation remained negative.

In such conditions it was obviously rare for a woman to
be able to act or simply to make her presence felt. In the
working classes economic oppression nullified the inequality
of the sexes, but it deprived the individual of all opportunity;
among the nobility and the bourgeoisie the female sex as such
was browbeaten: woman had only a parasitic existence; she
had little education; only under exceptional circumstances
could she envisage and carry out any concrete project. Queens
and regents had this rare pleasure: their sovereignty lifted
them above their sex. In France the Salic law forbade women
to succeed to the throne; but beside their husbands, or after

[1] Casanova writes with amusing asperity about the efforts of
the Empress Maria Theresa to advance morality by legislation
and cites the thieving activities of 'a legion of vile spies... the
Commissaries of Chastity'. (*Memoirs*, vol. III.)—Tr.

their death, they sometimes played a great role, as did, for example, St. Clotilda, St. Radegonde, and Blanche of Castile. Living in a convent made women independent of man: certain abbesses wielded great power; Héloïse gained fame as an abbess as much as for her love. From the mystical relation that bound them to God, feminine souls drew all the inspiration and the strength of a male soul; and the respect paid them by society enabled them to accomplish difficult enterprises. Joan of Arc's adventure had in it something of the miraculous, and besides it was only a brief escapade. But the story of St. Catherine of Siena is significant; in the midst of a quite normal existence she created in Siena a great reputation by her active benevolence and by the visions that testified to her intense inner life; thus she acquired the authority necessary in exhorting those condemned to death, in bringing back wanderers, and in allaying quarrels between families and cities. She had the support of a society that recognized itself in her, and thus it was that she could fulfil her mission of pacification, preaching from city to city submission to the Pope, keeping up extensive correspondence with bishops and rulers, and in the end being chosen by Florence as ambassadress to go to seek out the Pope in Avignon. Queens by divine right, and saints by their dazzling virtues, were assured a social support that enabled them to act on an equality with men. From other women, in contrast, only a modest silence was called for.

On the whole, men in the Middle Ages held a rather unfavourable opinion of women. The court poets, to be sure, exalted love; in the *Roman de la Rose* young men were urged to devote themselves to the service of the ladies. But opposed to this literature (inspired by that of the troubadours) were the writings of bourgeois inspiration, which attacked women with malignancy: fables, comedies, and lays charged them with laziness, coquetry, and lewdness. Their worst enemies were the clerics, who laid the blame on marriage. The Church had made it a sacrament and yet had forbidden it to the Christian *élite*: there lay a contradiction which was at the source of the 'quarrel of women'. Various clerics wrote 'lamentations' and diatribes about woman's failings, the martyrdom of man in marriage, and so on; and their opponents tried to prove woman's superiority. This quarrel went on through the fifteenth century, until for the first time we see a woman take up her pen in defence of her sex when Christine de Pisan made a lively attack on the clerics in her *Epitre au Dieu d'Amour*. Later she maintained that if little girls were as well taught, they would 'understand the subtleties of all the arts and sciences' as well as boys. The truth of the matter was that this dispute concerned women only indirectly. No one dreamed of demanding for them a social role different from the one they had. It was rather a matter of contrasting the life of the cleric with the married state; that is to say, it was a male problem raised by the Church's ambiguous attitude in regard to marriage. This conflict Luther solved by refusing to accept the celibacy of priests. The situation of woman was not affected by that literary war; the 'quarrel' was a secondary phenomenon reflecting social attitudes but not changing them.

Woman's legal status remained almost unchanged from the beginning of the fifteenth century to the nineteenth, but in the privileged classes her actual situation did improve. The Italian Renaissance was an individualistic epoch favourable for the emergence of strong personalities, regardless of sex. Women were powerful sovereigns, military fighters and leaders, artists, writers, and musicians. Most of these women of distinction were courtesans, free in spirit, manners, and finances, and their crimes and orgies are legendary. In later centuries the same licence marked those women of rank or fortune who could escape the harsh common morality of the times. Apart from queens—Catherine de Medici, Elizabeth, Isabella—and such saints as Theresa and Catherine, who showed what women could achieve under favourable circumstances, the positive accomplishments of women were few, for education and other advantages were largely denied them through the sixteenth century.

In the seventeenth century women of leisure applied themselves to arts and letters, playing an important part in the salons as culture spread in higher social levels. In France Mme de Rambouillet, Mme de Sévigné, and others enjoyed vast renown, and elsewhere Queen Christine, Mlle de Schurman, and others were similarly celebrated. Through such qualities and prestige, women of rank or reputation began to penetrate into the world of men, finally showing in the person of Mme de Maintenon how great an influence can be exerted in affairs of state by an adroit woman, working behind the scenes. And a few personalities escaped from the bourgeois repression to make their mark in the world; a hitherto un-

129

E

known species appeared: the actress. The first woman was seen on the stage in 1545. Even at the beginning of the seventeenth century most actresses were actors' wives, but later they became independent in career as in private life. The courtesan attained her most accomplished incarnation in Ninon de Lenclos, who carried her independence and liberty to the highest extreme then permitted to a woman.

In the eighteenth century woman's freedom continued to increase. The mores were still strict: the young girl got only a sketchy education; and she was married off or sent into a convent without being consulted. The rising middle class imposed a strict morality upon wives. But women of the world led extremely licentious lives, and the upper middle class was contaminated by such examples; neither the convent nor the home could contain woman. Once again, for the majority this liberty remained abstract and negative: there was little more than the search for pleasure. But the intelligent and ambitious created opportunities. The salon took on new splendour; women protected and inspired the writer and made up his public; they studied philosophy and science and set up laboratories of physics and chemistry. In politics the names of Mme de Pompadour and Mme du Barry indicate woman's power; they really controlled the State. Actresses and women of gallantry enjoyed vast renown. Thus throughout the Old Regime the cultural sphere was the one most accessible to women who attempted to do something. Yet none ever reached the heights of a Dante or a Shakespeare, a fact that is explained by the general mediocrity of their situation. Culture was never an attribute of any but the feminine *élite*, never of the mass; and it is often from the mass that masculine genius has arisen. Even the privileged were surrounded by obstacles, and while nothing hindered the flights of a St. Theresa or a Catherine the Great, a thousand circumstances conspired against the woman writer. In *A Room of One's Own* Virginia Woolf contrasts the meagre and restricted life of an imaginary sister of Shakespeare with his life of learning and adventure. It was only in the eighteenth century that a middle-class woman, Mrs. Aphra Behn, a widow, earned her living by her pen like a man. Others followed her example, but even in the nineteenth century they were often obliged to hide. They did not have even 'a room of their own'; that is to say, they did not enjoy that material independence which is one of the necessary conditions for inner liberty. In England,

Virginia Woolf remarks, women writers have always aroused hostility.

In France things were somewhat more favourable, because of the alliance between the social and the intellectual life, but, in general, opinion was hostile to 'bluestockings'. From the Renaissance on, women of rank and of wit, with Erasmus and other men, wrote in defence of women. Marguerite of Navarre did most for the cause, proposing, in opposition to licentious mores, an ideal of sentimental mysticism and of chastity without prudery that would reconcile marriage with love for the honour and happiness of women. The enemies of woman were not silent, of course. They revived the old arguments of the Middle Ages, and published *Alphabets* with a fault of woman for every letter. A libertine literature—*Cabinet Satyrique* and the like—arose to attack feminine follies, while the religious cited St. Paul, the Church Fathers, and Ecclesiastes for woman's disparagement.

The very successes of women aroused new attacks against them: the affected women called *précieuses* alienated public opinion; the *Précieuses ridicules* and *Femmes savantes* were applauded, though Molière was no enemy of women: he sharply attacked enforced marriage, demanding freedom of sentiment for the young girl and respect and independence for the wife. Bossuet preached against woman, and Boileau wrote satires, arousing fiery defenders of the sex. Poulain de la Barre, the leading feminist of the time, published in 1673 *De l'egalité des deux sexes*. Men, he thought, used their superior strength to favour their own sex, and women acquiesced by habit in their dependence. They had never had a fair chance—neither liberty nor education. Thus they could not be judged by past performance, he argued, and nothing indicated that they were inferior to men. He demanded real education for women.

The eighteenth century was also divided in the matter. Some writers tried to prove that woman had no immortal soul. Rousseau dedicated woman to husband and to maternity, thus speaking for the middle class. 'Women's entire education should be relative to men,' he said; '. . . woman was made to yield to man and to put up with his injustice.' The democratic and individualist ideal of the eighteenth century, however, was favourable to women; to most philosophers they seemed to be human beings equal to those belonging to the stronger sex. Voltaire denounced the injustice of woman's lot. Diderot felt that her inferiority had been

131

largely *made* by society. Montesquieu believed paradoxically that 'it is against reason and nature that women be in control of the home . . . not at all that they govern an empire'. Helvétius showed that the absurdity of woman's education is what creates the inferiority of woman. But it was Mercier who almost alone, in his *Tableau de Paris,* waxed indignant at the misery of working-women and thus opened the fundamental question of feminine labour. Condorcet wanted women to enter political life, considering them equal to man if equally educated. 'The more women have been enslaved by the laws,' he said, 'the more dangerous has been their empire . . . It would decline if it were less to women's interest to maintain it, if it ceased to be their sole means of defending themselves and escaping from oppression.'

CHAPTER V

SINCE THE FRENCH REVOLUTION: THE JOB AND THE VOTE

IT might well have been expected that the Revolution would change the lot of woman. It did nothing of the sort. That middle-class Revolution was respectful of middle-class institutions and values and it was accomplished almost exclusively by men. It is important to exphazize the fact that throughout the Old Regime it was the women of the working classes who as a sex enjoyed most independence. Woman had the right to manage a business and she had all the legal powers necessary for the independent pursuit of her calling. She shared in production as seamstress, laundress, burnisher, shopkeeper, and so on ; she worked either at home or in small places of business ; her material independence permitted her a great freedom of behaviour: a woman of the people could go out, frequent taverns, and dispose of her body as she saw fit almost like a man ; she was her husband's associate and equal. It was on the economic, not on the sexual plane that she suffered oppression. In the country the peasant woman took a considerable part in farm labour ; she was treated as a servant ; frequently she did not eat at the table with her husband and sons, she slaved harder than they did, and the burdens of maternity added to her fatigue. But as in ancient agricultural societies, being necessary to man she was respected by him ; their goods, their interests, their cares were all in common ; she exercised great authority in the home. These are the women who, out of the midst of their hard life, might have been able to assert themselves and demand their rights ; but a tradition of timidity and of submissiveness weighed on them. The *cahiers* of the States-General contained but few feminine claims, and these were restricted to keeping men out of women's occupations. And certainly women were to be seen beside their men in demonstrations and riots ; these women went to seek at Versailles 'the baker, his wife, and his little journeyman'. But it was not the common people who led the Revolution and enjoyed its fruits.

As for the middle-class women, some ardently took up the cause of liberty, such as Mme Roland and Lucile Desmoulins. One of them who had a profound influence on the course of events was Charlotte Corday when she assassinated Marat. There was some feminist agitation. Olympe de Gouges proposed in 1789 a 'Declaration of the Rights of Woman', equivalent to the 'Declaration of the Rights of Man', in which she asked that all masculine privilege be abolished; but she perished before long on the scaffold. Short-lived journals appeared, and fruitless efforts were made by a few women to undertake political activities.

In 1790 the right of the eldest and the masculine prerogative in inheritance were abolished; girls and boys became equals in this respect. In 1792 a law was passed establishing divorce and thus relaxing matrimonial bonds. But these were only insignificant victories. Middle-class women were too well integrated in the family to feel any definite solidarity as a sex; they did not constitute a separate caste capable of imposing claims: economically they led a parasitic existence. Thus it was that while women who, in spite of their sex, could have taken part in events were prevented from doing so on account of their class, those belonging to the active class were condemned to stand aside as being women. When economic power falls into the hands of the workers, then it will become possible for the working-woman to win rights and privileges that the parasitic woman, noble or middle-class, has never obtained.

During the Revolution woman enjoyed a liberty that was anarchic. But when society underwent reorganization, she was firmly enslaved anew. From the feminist point of view, France was ahead of other countries; but unfortunately for the modern Frenchwoman, her status was decided during a military dictatorship; the Code Napoléon, fixing her lot for a century, greatly retarded her emancipation. Like all military men, Napoleon preferred to see in woman only a mother; but as heir to a bourgeois revolution, he was not one to disrupt the structure of society and give the mother pre-eminence over the wife. He forbade the investigation of paternity; he set stern conditions for the unwed mother and the natural child. The married woman herself, however, did not find refuge in her dignity as mother; the feudal paradox was perpetuated. Girl and wife were deprived of the attribute of citizenship, which prevented them from practising law and acting as guardian. But the celibate woman, the spinster, enjoyed full civil powers, while marriage preserved the old dependency. The wife owed *obedience* to her husband; he could have her condemned to solitary confinement for adultery and get a divorce from her; if he killed her, caught in the act, he was excusable in the eyes of the law; whereas the husband was liable to penalty only if he brought a concubine into the home, and it was in this case only that the wife could obtain a divorce from him. The man decided where to live and had much more authority over the children than did the wife; and, except where the wife managed a commercial enterprise, his authorization was necessary for her to incur obligations. Her person and property were both under rigorous marital control.

During the nineteenth century jurisprudence only reinforced the rigours of the Code. Divorce was abolished in 1826, and was not restored until 1884, when it was still very difficult to obtain. The middle class was never more powerful, but it was uneasy in its authority, mindful of the menaces implied in the industrial revolution. Woman was declared made for the family, not for politics; for domestic cares and not for public functions. Auguste Comte declared that there were radical differences, physical and moral, between male and female which separated them profoundly, especially in the human race. Femininity was a kind of 'prolonged infancy' that set woman aside from 'the ideal of the race' and enfeebled her mind. He foresaw the total abolition of female labour outside the home. In morality and love woman might be set up as superior; but man acted, while she remained in the home without economic or political rights.

Balzac expressed the same ideal in more cynical terms. In the *Physiologie du mariage* he wrote: 'The destiny of woman and her sole glory are to make beat the hearts of men . . . she is a chattel and properly speaking only a subsidiary to man.' Here he speaks for the anti-feminist middle class, in reaction against both eighteenth-century licence and the threatening progressive ideas of the time. Balzac showed that bourgeois marriage where love is excluded naturally leads to adultery, and he exhorted husbands to keep a firm rein, deny their wives all education and culture, and keep them as unattractive as possible. The middle class followed this programme, confining women to the kitchen and the home, closely watching their behaviour, keeping them wholly dependent. In compensation they were held in honour and treated with the most exquisite politeness. 'The married woman is a slave whom one must be able to set on a throne,' said **Balzac**. She must be yielded to in trifles, given first place ; instead of making her carry burdens as among primitives one must rush forward to relieve her of any painful task and of all care—and at the same time of all responsibility. Most bourgeois women accepted this gilded confinement, and the few who complained were unheard. Bernard Shaw remarks that it is easier to put chains on men than to remove them, if the chains confer benefits. The middle-class woman clung to her chains because she clung to the privileges of her class. Freed from the male, she would have to work for a living ; she felt no solidarity with working-women, and she believed that the emancipation of bourgeois women would mean the ruin of her class.

The march of history, however, was not stopped by such obstinate resistance ; the coming of the machine destroyed landed property and furthered the emancipation of the working class along with that of women. All forms of socialism, wresting woman away from the family, favour her liberation: Plato envisioned a communal regime and promised women an autonomy in it such as they enjoyed in Sparta. With the utopian socialisms of Saint-Simon, Fourier, and Cabet was born the utopia of the 'free woman' ; the slavery of worker and of woman was to be abolished, for women like men were human beings. Unfortunately this reasonable idea did not prevail in the school of Saint-Simonism. Fourier, for example, confused the emancipation of women with the rehabilitation of the flesh, demanding for every individual the right to yield to the call of passion and wishing to replace marriage with love ; he considered woman not as a person but only in her amorous function. Cabet promised the complete equality of the sexes, but he restricted woman's share in politics. Others demanded better education for women rather than emancipation. The lofty notion of woman the regenerating influence persisted through the nineteenth century and appears in Victor Hugo. But woman's cause was rather discredited by the ineptitude of woman's partisans. Clubs, magazines, delegations, movements like 'Bloomerism' —all went down in ridicule. The most intelligent women of the time, like Mme de Staël and George Sand, remained apart from these movements while fighting their own battles for freedom. But feminism was favoured in general by the reform movement of the nineteenth century because it sought justice in equality. Proudhon was a remarkable exception. He broke the alliance between feminism and socialism, relegating the honest woman to the home and to dependence on the male, and attempting to demonstrate her inferiority. 'Housewife or harlot' was the choice he offered. But like all anti-feminists he addressed ardent litanies to 'the true woman', slave and mirror of the male. In spite of this devotion, he was unable to make his own wife happy: the letters of Mme Proudhon are one long lament.

These theoretical debates did not affect the course of events: rather they were a hesitant reflection of things taking place. Woman regained an economic importance that had been lost since prehistoric times, because she escaped from the hearth and assumed in the factory a new part in production. It was the machine that made possible this upheaval, for the difference in physical strength between male and female workers was to a large extent annulled. As the swift growth of industry demanded a larger working force than the males alone could furnish, the collaboration of women became necessary. That was the grand revolution of the nineteenth century, which transformed the lot of woman and opened for her a new era. Marx and Engels gauged its whole range, and they promised women a liberation implied in that of the proletariat. In fact, 'woman and the worker have this in common: that they are both oppressed,' said Bebel. And both would escape together from oppression, thanks to the importance their work would take on through technological evolution. Engels showed that the lot of woman has been closely tied to the history of private property; a calamity put the patriarchate in place of the matrilineal regime and enslaved woman to the patrimony. But the industrial revolution was the counterpart of that loss of rights and would lead to feminine emancipation. His conclusion has already been quoted (page 74).

At the beginning of the nineteenth century woman was more shamefully exploited than were male workers. Labour at home constituted what the English called the 'sweating system'; in spite of constant toil, the working-woman did not earn enough to satisfy her needs. Jules Simon in *L'Ouvrière* and even the conservative Leroy-Beaulieu in *Le Travail des femmes au XIX*, published in 1873, denounced odious abuses; the latter says that more than two hundred thousand women workers in France earned less than fifty centimes a day. It is understandable that they made haste to get out into the factories; besides, it was not long before nothing was left to do outside the workshops except needlework, laundering, and housework—all slave's work, earning famine wages. Even lacemaking, millinery, and the like were monopolized by the factories. By way of compensation, there were large opportunities for employment in the cotton, wool, and silk industries; women were used especially in spinning- and weaving-mills. The employers often preferred them to men. 'They do better work for less pay.' This cynical formula lights up the drama of feminine labour. For it is through labour that woman has conquered her dignity as a human being; but it was a remarkably hard-won and protracted conquest.

Spinning and weaving were done under lamentably unhygienic conditions. 'In Lyon,' wrote Blanqui, 'in the lace workshops some of the women are compelled to work almost hanging on straps while they use both hands and feet.' In 1831 the silk workers laboured in summer from three o'clock in the morning until dark, and in winter from five to eleven at night, seventeen hours a day, 'in workshops that were often unwholesome and where the sunlight never penetrated,' as Norbert Truquin said. 'Half of these young girls became consumptive before finishing their apprenticeship. When they complained, they were accused of putting on airs.'[1]

Moreover, the male employees took advantage of the young working-girls. 'To attain their ends, they made use of the most shocking means: want and hunger,' said the anonymous author of the *Vérité sur les événements de Lyon*. Sometimes women did farm work in addition to their labour at the factory. They were cynically exploited. In a note in *Das Kapital* Marx relates the following: 'The manufacturer, Mr. E., informed me that he employed women only at his power looms, that he gave preference to married women and among them to those who had families at home to support, because these were more attentive and docile than the unmarried and had to work to the very end of their strength in order to obtain the necessaries of life for their families.' And Marx adds: 'Thus it is that woman's true qualities are warped to her disadvantage, and all the moral and delicate elements in her nature become the means for enslaving her and making her suffer.' Summing up Marx and commenting on Bebel, G. Derville wrote: 'Pet or beast of burden: such is woman almost exclusively today. Supported by man when she does

[1] N. TRUQUIN, *Mémoires et aventures d'un prolétaire*. Quoted from E. DOLLEANS, *Histoire du mouvement ouvrier*, vol. I.

not work, she is still supported by him when she works herself to death.' The situation of the working-woman was so deplorable that Sismondi and Blanqui demanded that women be denied employment in the workrooms. The reason for their condition was in part because women at first did not know how to defend themselves and organize themselves in unions. Women's 'associations' dated from 1848, and at the beginning these were associations of industrial workers. The movement advanced very slowly, as these figures show:

In 1905, there were 69,405 women out of 781,392 unionized workers ; in 1908, 88,906 out of 957,120 ; in 1912, 92,336 out of 1,064,413.

In 1920, there were 329,016 working-women and female employees unionized out of 1,580,967 workers ; and among women farm labourers only 36,193 unionized out of a total of 1,083,957. In all, there were 292,000 women unionized out of a total of 3,076,585 union workers. It was a tradition of resignation and submission, a lack of solidarity and collective consciousness, that left them thus disarmed before the new opportunities that were opening up for them.

The result of this attitude was that female labour was slowly and tardily regulated. Only in 1874 did the law intervene ; and yet, in spite of the campaigns waged under the Empire, there were only two provisions concerning women: one forbade night work for female minors and required that they be allowed to rest on Sundays and holidays, and their workday was limited to twelve hours ; as for women over twenty-one, no more was done than to forbid underground labour in mines and quarries. The first charter for feminine labour was dated November 2nd, 1892 ; it forbade night work and limited the factory day ; but it left the door open for all kinds of evasion. In 1900 the day was limited to ten hours ; in 1905 the weekly day of rest was made obligatory ; in 1907 the working-woman was granted free handling of her income ; in 1909 leave with pay was guaranteed to women for childbirth ; in 1911 the provisions of 1892 were strongly reasserted ; in 1913 the periods of rest before and after childbirth were regulated in detail, and dangerous and excessive forms of labour were forbidden. Little by little social legislation was set up and feminine labour was surrounded with hygienic precautions: chairs were required for shop-assistants, long hours at outside displays were forbidden, and so on. The International Labour Office led to international conventions of the sanitary conditions of women's labour, leave to be granted for pregnancy, and so forth.

A second consequence of the resigned inertia of female workers appeared in the wages with which they had to be satisfied. The phenomenon of low wages for women has been variously explained, and it is due to a complex of factors. It is not enough to say that women's needs are less than those of men: that is only justification by afterthought. The truth is, rather, that women, as we have seen, were unable to defend themselves against their exploiters; they had to meet the competition of the prisons, which threw on the market products fabricated without expense for labour; and they competed with one another. It must be remarked in addition that woman was seeking emancipation through labour in a society in which the family continued to exist: tied to her father's or her husband's hearth, she was most often satisfied to bring extra money into the family exchequer; she worked outside the family, but for it; and since the working-woman did not have to provide for the whole of her needs, she was led to accept remuneration far below what a man required. Since a significant number of women were thus content with depreciated wages, the pay of women in general was of course set at a level most advantageous to the employer.

The woman worker in France, according to a study made in the years 1889-93, received only half the pay of a man for a day's work equal to that of a man. According to the investigation of 1908, the highest hourly wages of workers at home did not exceed twenty centimes per hour and went as low as five centimes; it was impossible for a woman thus exploited to live without charity or a protector. In America in 1918 a woman got only half a man's wage. At about this time in the German mines a woman got approximately twenty-five per cent less than a man for digging the same amount of coal. Between 1911 and 1943 women's wages in France were raised a little more rapidly than the men's, but they remained definitely lower.

If employers warmly welcomed women because of the low wages they would accept, this same fact gave rise to opposition from the male workers. Between the cause of the proletariat and that of women there was no such immediate solidarity as Bebel and Engels claimed. The problem was presented in somewhat the same way as that of the Negro labourer in the United States. The most oppressed minorities

140

of a society are readily used by the oppressors as a weapon against the whole class to which they belong; thus these minorities seem to their class at first to be enemies, and a more profound comprehension of the situation is needed in order that the interests of blacks and whites, of women workers and men workers, may achieve unity instead of being opposed to each other. It is understandable that male workers at first saw a formidable danger in this cut-rate competition and that they exhibited hostility to it. Only when women have been integrated into the life of trade-unionism have they been able to defend their own interests and cease endangering those of the working class as a whole.

Despite all these difficulties, progress continued in the field of female labour. In 1900 there were still 900,000 home workers in France making clothes, leather goods, funeral wreaths, bags, beadwork, and novelties; but the number has subsequently diminished considerably. In 1906, 42 per cent of women of working age (between eighteen and sixty) were employed in farming, industry, business, banking, insurance, office work, and the learned professions. According to a census taken just before the last war, we find that of all women from eighteen to sixty, about 42 per cent in France are workers, 37 per cent in Finland, 34.2 in Germany, 27.7 in India, 26.9 in England, 19.2 in Holland, and 17.7 per cent in the United States. But in France and India the figures are high because of the importance of rural labour. Outside the peasantry, there were in France in 1940 about 500,000 female heads of businesses, 1,000,000 women employees, 2,000,000 women workers, and 1,500,000 self-employed or unemployed women. Among the workers there were 650,000 domestics; 1,200,000 worked in the finishing industries (44,000 in textiles, 315,000 in clothing, 380,000 in home dressmaking). Regarding women in commerce, the learned professions, and the public services, France, England, and the United States are of about the same rank.

One of the basic problems of woman, as we have seen, is the reconciliation of her reproductive role and her part in productive labour. The fundamental fact that from the beginning of history doomed woman to domestic work and prevented her taking part in the shaping of the world was her enslavement to the generative function. In female animals there is a physiological and seasonal rhythm that assures the economizing of their strength; in women, on the contrary, between puberty and the menopause nature sets no limits to

141

the number of her pregnancies. Certain civilizations forbid early marriage, and it is said that in certain Indian tribes a rest of at least two years between childbirth is assured to women; but in general, woman's fecundity has been unregulated for many centuries. Contraceptives have been in existence since antiquity,[1] usually to be used by the woman: potions, suppositories, vaginal tampons; but they remained the secret of prostitutes and doctors. Perhaps this secret was known to those Roman women of the decline whose sterility was attacked by the satirists. But contraceptives were practically unknown to the Middle Ages in Europe; scarcely a trace of them is to be found up to the eighteenth century. For many women life in those times was an uninterrupted succession of pregnancies; even women of easy virtue paid for their licentious lovemaking by frequent childbearing.

At certain epochs man has strongly felt the need to reduce the size of the population; but at the same time nations have feared becoming weak. In times of crisis and misery the birth rate may have been reduced by late marriage, but it remained the general rule to marry young and have as many children as the woman could produce; infant mortality alone reduced the number of living children. As early as the seventeenth century the Abbé de Pure[2] protested against the 'love dropsy' to which women were condemned; and Mme de Sévigné advised her daughter to avoid too frequent pregnancies. But it was in the eighteenth century that Malthusianism developed in France. First the wealthy classes, then the population generally found it reasonable to limit the number of children according to the means of the parents, and contraceptive measures began to be used. In 1778 the demographer

---

[1] 'The earliest known reference to birth-control methods appears to be an Egyptian papyrus of about 2000 B.C., which recommends application in the vagina of a bizarre mixture of crocodile excrement, honey, soda, and a gummy substance,' according to P. ARIES, *Histoire des populations françaises*. [In NORMAN HIMES'S *Medical History of Contraception* (1936), the date of this papyrus, found at Kahun in 1889, is given as about 1850 B.C. Himes presents photographs of this historic document and discusses the chemical nature of the substances mentioned.—TR.] Persian physicians at the time of the Middle Ages knew thirty-one recipes, of which only nine were to be used by the male. Soranos, at the time of Hadrian, prescribed that the woman who did not wish to conceive should, at the time of ejaculation, 'hold her breath, draw her body back a little so that the sperm could not penetrate into the *os uteri*, rise immediately, squat down, and bring on sneezing'.

[2] In the *Précieuse* (1656).

Moreau wrote: 'Rich women are not the only ones who regard the propagation of the species as an old-fashioned imposition; already these disastrous secrets, unknown to all animals but man, have reached the country; nature is deceived even in the villages.' The practice of *coitus interruptus* spread first among the middle classes, then among country people and the workers; the already existing anti-venereal protection became a contraceptive that found wisespread use especially after the discovery of vulcanization, towards 1840.[1] In Anglo-Saxon countries 'birth control' is officially sanctioned and numerous methods have been developed for dissociating those two formerly inseparable functions: the sexual and the reproductive. Medical research in Vienna and elsewhere, in setting forth precisely the mechanism of conception and the conditions favourable to it, has indicated also the ways of avoiding it. In France contraceptive propaganda and the sale of pessaries and other supplies are forbidden; but 'birth control' is none the less widely practised.

As for abortion, it is nowhere officially sanctioned by the laws. Roman law accorded no especial protection to embryonic life; it regarded the *nasciturus* (to be born) as a part of the maternal body, not as a human being. In the period of the decline abortion seemed to be a normal practice, and even the legislator who wished to encourage childbearing did not venture to forbid it. If a wife rejected her infant against her husband's will, he could have her punished, but it was her disobedience that constituted the offence. Throughout the whole of Oriental and Greco-Roman civilization abortion was permissible.

Christianity revolutionized moral ideas in this matter by endowing the embryo with a soul; for then abortion became a crime against the fetus itself. According to St. Augustine, 'Any woman who acts in such a way that she cannot give birth to as many children as she is capable of makes herself guilty of that many murders, just as with the woman who tries to injure herself after conception.' Ecclesiastical law developed gradually, with interminable discussions on such questions as when the soul actually enters the body of the fetus. St. Thomas and others set the time of animation at about the fortieth day for males and the eightieth day for females. Different degrees of guilt were attached to abortion

[1] 'About 1930 an American firm sold twenty million protective items in one year. Fifteen American factories produced a million and a half of them per day.' (P. Ariès.)

in the Middle Ages according to when it was performed and why: 'There is a great difference between the poor woman who destroys her infant on account of the difficulty of supporting it, and her who has no aim other than hiding the crime of fornication,' said the book of penitence. An edict of Henri II in 1556 was the basis for regarding abortion as murder and punishable with death. The Code of 1791 excused the woman but punished her accomplices. In the nineteenth century the idea that abortion is murder disappeared; it was regarded rather as a crime against the State. The French law of 1810 forbade it absolutely, with heavy penalties; but physicians always practised it whenever it was a question of saving the mother's life. The law was too strict and at the end of the century few arrests were made and still fewer convictions reached. New laws were passed in 1932 and 1939, with some variations in the penalties; and in 1941 abortion was decreed a crime against the safety of the State. In other countries the crime and its punishment have been variously regarded, but in general laws and courts have been much more lenient with the woman having the abortion than with her accomplices. The Catholic Church, however, has in no way softened its rigour, and in 1917 the code of canon law called for the excommunication of all concerned in an abortion. The Pope has again quite recently declared that as between the life of the mother and that of the infant, the former must be sacrificed: of course the mother, being baptized, can gain entrance to heaven—oddly enough, hell never enters these calculations—whereas the fetus is doomed to limbo for eternity.[1] Abortion has been officially recognized during a brief period only: in Germany before Nazism, and in Russia before 1936. But in spite of religion and the law, it holds a place of considerable importance in all countries. In France

[1] We will return in Book Two to the discussion of this view, noting here only that the Catholics are far from keeping to the letter of St. Augustine's doctrine. The confessor whispers to the young fiancée the day before the wedding that she can behave in no matter what fashion with her husband from the moment that intercourse is properly completed; positive methods of birth control, including *coitus interruptus,* are forbidden, but one has the right to make use of the calendar established by the Viennese sexologists (the 'rhythm') and commit the act of which the sole recognized end is reproduction on days when conception is supposed to be impossible for the woman. There are spiritual advisers who even give this calendar to their flock. As a matter of fact, there are plenty of Christian mothers who have only two or three children though they did not completely sever marital relations after the last accouchement.

abortions number each year from 800,000 to 1,000,000—
about as many as there are births—two-thirds of those
aborted being married women, many already having one or
two children.

Thus it is, then, that in spite of prejudices, opposition, and
the survival of an outdated morality, we have witnessed the
passage from free fecundity to a fecundity controlled by the
State or by individuals. Progress in obstetrical science has considerably reduced the dangers of confinement; and the pain
of childbirth is reduced. At this time—March 1949—legislation has been passed in England requiring the use of certain
anaesthetic methods; they are in general application in the
United States and are beginning to spread in France. Artificial insemination completes the evolutionary advance that will
enable humanity to master the reproductive function. These
changes are of tremendous importance for woman in part-
ticular; she can reduce the number of her pregnancies and
make them a rationally integral part of her life, instead of
being their slave. During the nineteenth century woman in
her turn emancipated herself from nature; she gained mastery of her own body. Now protected in large part from the
slavery of reproduction, she is in a position to assume the
economic role that is offered her and will assure her of complete independence.

The evolution of woman's condition is to be explained by
the concurrent action of these two factors: sharing in productive labour and being freed from slavery to reproduction.
As Engels has foreseen, woman's social and political status
was necessarily to be transformed. The feminist movement,
sketched out in France by Condorcet, in England by Mary
Wollstonecraft in her *Vindication of the Rights of Woman*,
and taken up again at the beginning of the nineteenth century
by the Saint-Simonists, had been unable to accomplish definite
results, as it lacked concrete bases. But now, with woman in
industry and out of the home, her demands began to take on
full weight. They were to make themselves heard at the very
centre of the bourgeoisie. In consequence of the rapid development of industrial civilization, landed property lost importance in relation to personal property, and the principle
of the family group lost force. The liquidity of capital
allowed its holder, instead of being possessed by it, to possess
it without reciprocal cares of ownership, and to dispose of it
at will. It was through the patrimony that woman had been
most strongly attached to her spouse; with the patrimony a

145

thing of the past, they were simply in juxtaposition, and not even their children united them with a firmness comparable to that of property interest. Thus the individual was to gain independence against the group.

This process was especially striking in America, where modern capitalism triumphed: divorce was to flourish and husband and wife seem no more than provisional associates. In France, where the rural population was a factor of importance and the Code Napoléon placed the married woman under guardianship, the process of evolution was bound to be slow. In 1884 divorce was restored, and the wife could obtain it if the husband committed adultery. In the matter of penology, however, the sex difference was retained: adultery was a legal offence only when committed by the wife. The power of trusteeship, granted with reservations in 1907, was fully obtained only in 1917. In 1912 the determination of natural paternity was authorized. The status of the married woman was modified in 1938 and 1942: the duty of obedience was then abrogated, though the father remained the head of the family. He determined the place of residence, though the wife could oppose his choice if she had good arguments. Her legal powers were increased; but in the confused statement: 'the married woman has full legal powers. These powers are limited only by the marriage contract and the law', the last part of the article contradicts the first. The equality of husband and wife was not yet an accomplished fact.

As for political rights, we can say that they were not easily achieved in France, England, and the United States. In 1867 John Stuart Mill made before the English Parliament the first speech ever officially presented in favour of votes for women. In his writings he imperiously demanded equality for woman and man within the family and in society at large. 'I am convinced that social arrangements which subordinate one sex to the other by law are bad in themselves and form one of the principal obstacles which oppose human progress; I am convinced that they should give place to a perfect equality.' Following him, Englishwomen organized politically under Mrs. Fawcett's leadership; the Frenchwomen rallied behind Maria Deraismes, who between 1868 and 1871 examined the lot of woman in a series of public conferences; she kept up a lively controversy with Alexandre Dumas *fils*, who gave the advice: 'Kill her' to the husband deceived by an unfaithful wife. Léon Richier, who was the true founder of feminism, produced in 1869 'The Rights of Woman' and organized the international congress on the subject, held in 1878. The question of the right to vote was not yet raised, the women limiting themselves to claiming civil rights. For nearly thirty years the movement remained very timid, in France as in England. Numerous groups were formed, but little was accomplished, because, as we have noted, women lacked solidarity as a sex.

The Socialist Congress of 1879 proclaimed the equality of the sexes, but feminism was a secondary interest since woman's emancipation was seen as depending on the liberation of the workers in general. In contrast, the bourgeois women were demanding new rights within the frame of existing social institutions and were far from being revolutionary. They favoured such virtuous reforms as the suppression of alcoholism, pornographic literature, and prostitution. A Feminist Congress was held in 1892, which gave its name to the movement but accomplished little else. A few advances were made, but in 1901 the question of votes for women was brought up for the first time before the Chamber of Deputies, by Viviani. The movement gained in importance, and in 1909 the French Union for Woman Suffrage was founded, with meetings and demonstrations organized by Mme Brunschwig. A woman-suffrage bill passed the Chamber in 1919, but failed in the Senate in 1922. The situation was complicated: to revolutionary feminism and the 'independent' feminism of Mme Brunschwig was added a Christian feminism, when Pope Benedict XV in 1919 pronounced in favour of votes for women. The Catholics felt that women in France represented a conservative and religious element; but the radicals feared precisely this. As late as 1932, extended debates took place in the Chamber and in the Senate, and all the anti-feminist arguments of a half-century were brought forward: the chivalrous thought that woman was on a pedestal and should stay there; the notion that the 'true woman' would remain at home and not lose her charm in voting, since she governs men without need of the ballot. And more seriously it was urged that politics would disrupt families; that women are different anyway—they do not perform military service. And it was asked: should prostitutes have the vote? Men were better educated; women would vote as told to by their husbands; if they wished to be free, let them first get free from their dressmakers; and anyway there were more women than men in France! Poor as these arguments were, it was necessary to wait until 1945 for the Frenchwomen to gain her political enfranchisement.

New Zealand gave woman full rights in 1893, and Australia followed in 1908. But in England and America the victory was difficult. Victorian England isolated woman in the home ; Jane Austen hid herself in order to write ; scientists proclaimed that woman was 'a subspecies destined only for reproduction'. Feminism was very timid until about 1903, when the Pankhurst family founded in London the Women's Social and Political Union, and feminist agitation took on a singular and militant character. For the first time in history women were to be seen taking action as women, which gives a special interest to the 'suffragette' adventure. For fifteen years they exerted pressure, at first without violence, marching with banners, invading meetings, provoking arrest, putting on hunger strikes, marching on Parliament with shawled workers and great ladies in line together, holding meetings, inciting further arrests, parading in columns miles long when votes on suffrage were being taken in Parliament. In 1912 more violent tactics were adopted: they burned houses, slashed pictures, trampled flowerbeds, threw stones at the police, overwhelmed Asquith and Sir Edward Grey with repeated deputations, interrupted public speeches. The war intervened. English women got the vote with restrictions in 1918, and the unrestricted vote in 1928. Their success was in large part due to the services they rendered during the war.

The American woman has from the first been more emancipated than her European sister. At the beginning of the nineteenth century women had to share with men the hard work of pioneering ; they fought at their side ; they were far fewer than the men, and this put a high value on them. But gradually their condition approached that of the women of the Old World ; they were highly regarded and dominant within the family, but social control remained entirely within male hands. Towards 1830 certain women began to lay claim to political rights ; they undertook a campaign in favour of the Negroes. Lucretia Mott, the Quakeress, founded an American feminist association, and at a convention in 1840 there was issued a manifesto of Quaker inspiration which set the tone for all American feminism. 'Man and women were created equals, provided by the Creator with inalienable rights . . . The government is set up only to safeguard these rights . . . Man has made a civic corpse of the married woman . . . He is usurping the prerogatives

148

of Jehovah who alone can assign human beings to their sphere of action.' Three years later Harriet Beecher Stowe wrote *Uncle Tom's Cabin,* which aroused public opinion in favour of the Negroes. Emerson and Lincoln supported the feminist movement. After the Civil War the feminists demanded in vain that the amendment giving the vote to the Negroes should give it also to women; taking advantage of an ambiguity, Susan B. Anthony and fourteen comrades voted in Rochester; she was fined one hundred dollars. In 1869 she founded the National Association for Woman Suffrage, and in the same year Wyoming gave women the vote. In 1893 Colorado followed, then in 1896 Idaho and Utah.

Progress was very slow thereafter; but economically woman succeeded better than in Europe. In 1900, 5,000,000 worked in the United States, including a large number in business and the learned professions. There were lawyers, doctors, professors, and as many as 3,373 woman pastors. Mary Baker Eddy founded the Christian Science Church. Women's clubs flourished, with about 2,000,000 members in 1900. But only nine states had given the vote to women. In 1913 the suffrage movement was organized on the militant English model. It was directed by two women: Doris Stevens and a Quakeress, Alice Paul, who arranged for meetings, parades, and other such manifestations. In Chicago for the first time a Woman's Party was founded. In 1917 the suffragettes stood at the doors of the White House, banners in hand, sometimes chained to ironwork so as not to be dislodged. They were arrested after six months but put on a hunger strike in prison and were soon released. After new disorders, a committee of the House met with one from the Woman's Party, and on January 10th, 1918, a constitutional amendment was passed. The Senate failed to pass it by two votes this time, but it did pass it a year later, and woman suffrage became the law of the land in 1920. Inter-American conferences led up to the signing in 1933 by nineteen American republics of a convention giving to women equality in all rights.

In Sweden also there existed a very important feminist movement. Invoking old Swedish tradition, the feminists demanded the right 'to education, to work, to liberty'. Women writers especially took the lead in this struggle, and it was the moral aspect of the problem that interested them at first. Grouped in powerful associations, they won over the liberals,

149

but ran up against the hostility of the conservatives. The Norwegian women won the suffrage in 1907, the Finnish women in 1906, but the Swedish women were to wait for years.

Latin countries, like Oriental countries, keep woman in subjection less by the rigour of the laws than by the severity of custom. In Italy, Fascism systematically hindered the progress of feminism. Seeking alliance with the Church, leaving the family untouched, and continuing a tradition of feminine slavery, Fascist Italy put woman in double bondage: to the public authorities and to her husband. The course of events was very different in Germany. A student named Hippel hurled the first manifesto of German feminism in 1790, and at the beginning of the nineteenth century a sentimental feminism was flourishing, akin to that of George Sand. In 1848 the first German woman feminist, Louise Otto, demanded for women the right to share in reforms of nationalist character and founded in 1865 a women's association. German Socialists favoured feminism, and Clara Zetkin in 1892 was among the party leaders. Female workers and Socialists formed a federation. Women took active part in the war, in 1914; and after the German defeat women got the vote and were active in political life. Rosa Luxemburg battled in the Spartacus group beside Liebknecht and was assassinated in 1919. The majority of German women came out for the party of order ; several sat in the Reichstag. Thus it was upon emancipated women that Hitler imposed anew the Napoleonic ideal: *'Küche, Kirche, Kinder.'* And he declared that 'the presence of a woman would dishonour the Reichstag'. As Nazism was anti-Catholic and anti-bourgeois, it gave a privileged place to motherhood, freeing women very largely from marriage through the protection it gave to unmarried mothers and to natural children. As in Sparta, woman depended upon the State much more than upon any individual man, and this gave her at once more and less independence than a middleclass woman would have living under a capitalist regime.

In Soviet Russia the feminist movement has made the most sweeping advances. It began among female student intellectuals at the end of the nineteenth century, and was even then connected with violent and revolutionary activity. During the Russo-Japanese War women replaced men in many kinds of work and made organized demands for equality. After 1905 they took part in political strikes and mounted the barricades ; and in 1917, a few days before the Revolution, they held a mass demonstration in St. Petersburg, demanding bread, peace, and the return of their men. They played a great part in the October rising and, later, in the battle against invasion. Faithful to Marxist tradition, Lenin bound the emancipation of women to that of the workers; he gave them political and economic equality.

Article 122 of the Constitution of 1936 states: 'In Soviet Russia woman enjoys the same rights as man in all aspects of economic, official, cultural, public, and political life.' And this has been more precisely stated by the Communist International, which makes the following demands: 'Social equality of man and woman before the law and in practical life. Radical transformation in conjugal rights and the family code. Recognition of maternity as a social function. Making a social charge of the care and education of children and adolescents. The organization of a civilizing struggle against the ideology and the traditions that make woman a slave.' In the economic field woman's conquests have been brilliant. She gets equal wages and participates on a large scale in production; and on account of this she has assumed a considerable social and political importance. There were in 1939 a great many women deputies to the various regional and local soviets, and more than two hundred sat in the Supreme Soviet of the U.S.S.R. Almost ten million are members of unions. Women constitute forty per cent of the workers and employees of the U.S.S.R.; and many women workers have become Stakhanovites. It is well known that Russian women took a great part in the last war, penetrating even into masculine aspects of production such as metallurgy and mining, rafting of timber, and railway construction. Women also distinguished themselves as aviators and parachute troops, and they formed partisan armies.

This activity of women in public life raised a difficult problem: what should be women's role in family life? During a whole period means had been sought to free her from domestic bonds. On November 16th, 1924, the Comintern in plenary session proclaimed: 'The Revolution is impotent as long as the notion of family and of family relations continues to exist.' The respect thereupon accorded to free unions, the facility of divorce, and the legalizing of abortions assured woman's liberty with relation to the male; laws concerning maternity leave, day nurseries, kindergartens, and the like alleviated the cares of maternity. It is difficult to make out through the haze of passionate and contradictory testimony just what woman's concrete situation really was; but what is sure is that today the requirements of repeopling the country have led to a different political view of the family: the family now appears as the elementary cell of society, and woman is both worker and housekeeper.[1] Sexual morality is of the strictest; the laws of 1936 and 1941 forbid abortion and almost suppress divorce; adultery is condemned by custom. Strictly subordinated to the State like all workers, strictly bound to the home, but having access to political life and to the dignity conferred by productive labour, the Russian woman is in a singular condition which would repay the close study that circumstances unfortunately prevent me from undertaking.

The United Nations Commission on the Status of Women at a recent session demanded that equality in rights of the two sexes be recognized in all countries, and it passed several motions tending to make this legal statute a concrete reality. It would seem, then, that the game is won. The future can only lead to a more and more profound assimilation of woman into our once masculine society.

If we cast a general glance over this history, we see several conclusions that stand out from it. And this one first of all: the whole of feminine history has been man-made. Just as in America there is no Negro problem, but rather a white problem;[2] just as 'anti-semitism is not a Jewish problem; it is our problem';[3] so the woman problem has always been a man's problem. We have seen why men had moral prestige along with physical strength from the start; they created values, mores, religions; never have women disputed this empire with them. Some isolated individuals—Sappho, Christine de Pisan, Mary Wollstonecraft, Olympe de Gouges—have protested against the harshness of their destiny, and occasionally mass demonstrations have been made; but neither the Roman matrons uniting against the Oppian law nor the Anglo-Saxon suffragettes could have succeeded with their pressure unless

[1] Olga Michakova, secretary of the central committee of the Communist Youth Organization, declared in 1944 in an interview: 'Soviet women should try to make themselves as attractive as nature and good taste permit. After the war they should dress like women and have a feminine gait . . . Girls are to be told to behave properly and walk like girls, and for this reason they will probably wear very narrow skirts which will compel a graceful carriage.'

[2] Cf. Myrdal, *The American Dilemma*.

[3] Cf. J. P. Sartre, *Réflexions sur la question juive*.

the men had been quite disposed to submit to it. Men have always held the lot of woman in their hands; and they have determined what it should be, not according to her interest, but rather with regard to their own projects, their fears, and their needs. When they revered the Goddess Mother, it was because they feared Nature; when the bronze tool allowed them to face Nature boldly, they instituted the patriarchate; then it became the conflict between family and State that defined woman's status; the Christian's attitude towards God, the world, and his own flesh was reflected in the situation to which he consigned her; what was called in the Middle Ages 'the quarrel of women' was a quarrel between clerics and laymen over marriage and celibacy; it was the social regime founded on private property that entailed the guardianship of the married woman, and it is the technological evolution accomplished by men that has emancipated the women of today. It was a transformation in masculine ethics that brought about a reduction in family size through birth control and partially freed woman from bondage to maternity. Feminism itself was never an autonomous movement; it was in part an instrument in the hands of politicians, in part an epiphenomenon reflecting a deeper social drama. Never have women constituted a separate caste, nor in truth have they ever as a sex sought to play a historic role. The doctrines that object to the advent of woman considered as flesh, life, immanence, the Other, are masculine ideologies in no way expressing feminine aspirations. The majority of women resign themselves to their lot without attempting to take any action; those who have tried to change it have intended not to be confined within the limits of their peculiarity and cause it to triumph, but to rise above it. When they have intervened in the course of world affairs, it has been in accord with men, in masculine perspectives.

This intervention, in general, has been secondary and episodic. The classes in which women enjoyed some economic independence and took part in production were the oppressed classes, and as women workers they were enslaved even more than the male workers. In the ruling classes woman was a parasite and as such was subjected to masculine laws. In both cases it was practically impossible for woman to take action. The law and the mores did not always coincide, and between them the equilibrium was established in such a manner that woman was never concretely free. In the ancient Roman Republic economic conditions gave the matron concrete powers, but she had no legal independence. Conditions were often similar for woman in peasant cizilizations and among the lower commercial middle class: mistress-servant in the house, but socially a minor. Inversely, in epochs of social disintegration woman is set free, but in ceasing to be man's vassal, she loses her fief; she has only a negative liberty, which is expressed in licence and dissipation. So it was with woman during the decline of Rome, the Renaissance, the eighteenth century, the Directory (1795-99). Sometimes she succeeded in keeping busy, but found herself enslaved; or she was set free and no longer knew what to do with herself. One remarkable fact among others is that the married woman had her place in society but enjoyed no rights therein; whereas the unmarried female, honest woman or prostitute, had all the legal capacities of a man, but up to this century was more or less excluded from social life.

From this opposition of legal rights and social custom has resulted, among other things, this curious paradox: free love is not forbidden by law, whereas adultery is an offence; but very often the young girl who 'goes wrong' is dishonoured, whereas the misconduct of the wife is viewed indulgently; and in consequence many young women from the seventeenth century to our own day have married in order to be able to take lovers freely. By means of this ingenious system the great mass of women is held closely in leading strings: exceptional circumstances are required if a feminine personality is to succeed in asserting itself between these two series of restraints, theoretical or concrete. The women who have accomplished works comparable to those of men are those exalted by the power of social institutions above all sexual differentiation. Queen Isabella, Queen Elizabeth, Catherine the Great were neither male nor female—they were sovereigns. It is remarkable that their femininity, when socially abolished, should have no longer meant inferiority: the proportion of queens who had great reigns is infinitely above that of great kings. Religion works the same transformation: Catherine of Siena, St. Theresa, quite beyond any physiological consideration, were sainted souls; the life they led, secular and mystic, their acts, and their writings rose to heights that few men have ever reached.

It is quite conceivable that if other women fail to make a deep impression upon the world, it is because they are tied down in their situation. They can hardly take a hand in affairs in other than a negative and oblique manner. Judith, Charlotte

Corday, Vera Zasulich were assassins; the *Frondeuses* were conspirators; during the Revolution, during the Commune, women battled beside the men against the established order. Against a liberty without rights, without powers, woman has been permitted to rise in refusal and revolt, while being forbidden to participate in positively constructive effort; at the most she may succeed in joining men's enterprises through an indirect road. Aspasia, Mme de Maintenon, the Princess des Ursins were counsellors who were listened to seriously— yet somebody had to be willing to listen to them. Men are glad to exaggerate the extent of these influences when they wish to convince woman that she has chosen the better part; but as a matter of fact, feminine voices are silent when it comes to concrete action. They have been able to stir up wars, not to propose battle tactics; they have directed politics only where politics is reduced to intrigue; the true control of the world has never been in the hands of women; they have not brought their influence to bear upon technique or economy, they have not made and unmade states, they have not discovered new worlds. Through them certain events have been set off, but the women have been pretexts rather than agents. The suicide of Lucretia has had value only as a symbol. Martyrdom remains open to the oppressed; during the Christian persecutions, on the morrow of social or national defeats, women have played this part of witness; but never has a martyr changed the face of the world. Even when women have started things and made demonstrations, these moves have taken on weight only when a masculine decision has effectively extended them. The American women grouped around Harriet Beecher Stowe aroused public opinion violently against slavery; but the true reasons for the War of Secession were not of a sentimental order. The 'woman's day' of March 8th, 1917, may perhaps have precipitated the Russian Revolution—but it was only a signal.

Most female heroines are oddities; adventuresses and originals notable less for the importance of their acts than for the singularity of their fates. Thus if we compare Joan of Arc, Mme Roland, Flora Tristan, with Richelieu, Danton, Lenin, we see that their greatness is primarily subjective; they are exemplary figures rather than historical agents. The great man springs from the masses and he is propelled onward by circumstances; the masses of women are on the margin of history, and circumstances are an obstacle for each individual, not a springboard. In order to change the face of the

155

world, it is first necessary to be firmly anchored in it; but the women who are firmly rooted in society are those who are in subjection to it; unless designated for action by divine authority—and then they have shown themselves to be as capable as men—the ambitious woman and the heroine are strange monsters. It is only since women have begun to feel themselves at home on the earth that we have seen a Rosa Luxemburg, a Mme Curie appear. They brilliantly demonstrate that it is not the inferiority of women that has caused their historical insignificance: it is rather their historical insignificance that has doomed them to inferiority.[1]

This fact is glaringly clear in the domain in which women have best succeeded in asserting themselves—that is, the domain of culture. Their lot has been deeply bound up with that of arts and letters; among the ancient Germans the functions of prophetess and priestess were already appropriate to women. Because of woman's marginal position in the world, men will turn to her when they strive through culture to go beyond the boundaries of their universe and gain access to something other than what they have known. Courtly mysticism, humanist curiosity, the taste for beauty which flourished in the Italian Renaissance, the preciosity of the seventeenth century, the progressive idealism of the eighteenth—all brought about under different forms an exaltation of femininity. Woman was thus the guiding star of poetry, the subject-matter of the work of art; her leisure allowed her to consecrate herself to the pleasures of the spirit: inspiration, critic, and public of the writer, she became his rival; she it was who often made prevail a mode of sensibility, an ethic that fed masculine hearts, and thus she intervened in her own destiny—the education of women was in large part a feminine conquest. And yet, however important this collective role of the intellectual woman may have been, the individual contributions have been in general of less value. It is because she has not been engaged in action that woman has had a privileged place in the domains of thought and of art; but art and thought have their living springs in action. To be situated at the margin of the world is not a position favourable for one

[1] It is remarkable that out of a thousand statues in Paris (excepting the queens that for a purely architectural reason form the corbel of the Luxembourg) there should be only ten raised to women. Three are consecrated to Joan of Arc. The others are statues of Mme de Ségur, George Sand, Sarah Bernhardt, Mme Boucicaut and the Baroness de Hirsch, Maria Deraismes, and Rosa Bonheur.

who aims at creating anew: here again, to emerge beyond the given, it is necessary first to be deeply rooted in it. Personal accomplishment is almost impossible in the human categories that are maintained collectively in an inferior situation. 'Where would you have one go, with skirts on?' Marie Bashkirtsev wanted to know. And Stendhal said: 'All the geniuses who are born *women* are lost to the public good.' To tell the truth, one is not born a genius: one becomes a genius; and the feminine situation has up to the present rendered this becoming practically impossible.

The anti-feminists obtain from the study of history two contradictory arguments: (1) women have never created anything great; and (2) the situation of woman has never prevented the flowering of great feminine personalities. There is bad faith in these two statements; the successes of a privileged few do not counterbalance or excuse the systematic lowering of the collective level; and that these successes are rare and limited proves precisely that circumstances are unfavourable for them. As has been maintained by Christine de Pisan, Poulain de la Barre, Condorcet, John Stuart Mill, and Stendhal, in no domain has woman ever really had her chance. That is why a great many woman today demand a new status; and once again their demand is not that they be exalted in their femininity: they wish that in themselves, as in humanity in general, transcendence may prevail over immanence; they wish to be accorded at last the abstract rights and concrete possibilities without the concurrence of which liberty is only a mockery.[1]

This wish is on the way to fulfilment. But the period in which we live is a period of transition; this world, which has always belonged to the men, is still in their hands; the institutions and the values of the patriarchal civilization still survive in large part. Abstract rights are far from being completely granted everywhere to women: in Switzerland they do not yet vote; in France the law of 1942 maintains in attenuated form the privileges of the husband. And abstract rights, as I have just been saying, have never sufficed to assure to woman

[1] Here again the anti-feminists take an equivocal line. Now, regarding abstract liberty as nothing, they expatiate on the great concrete role that the enslaved woman can play in the world—what, then, is she asking for? Again, they disregard the fact that negative licence opens no concrete possibilities, and they reproach women who are abstractly emancipated for not having produced evidence of their abilities.

a definite hold on the world: true equality between the two sexes does not exist even today.

In the first place, the burdens of marriage weigh much more heavily upon woman than upon man. We have noted that servitude to maternity has been reduced by the use—admitted or clandestine—of birth control; but the practice has not spread everywhere nor is it invariably used. Abortion being officially forbidden, many women either risk their health in unsupervised efforts to abort or find themselves overwhelmed by their numerous pregnancies. The care of children like the upkeep of the home is still undertaken almost exclusively by woman. Especially in France the anti-feminist tradition is so tenacious that a man would feel that he was lowering himself by helping with tasks hitherto assigned to women. The result is that it is more difficult for woman than for man to reconcile her family life with her role as worker. Whenever society demands this effort, her life is much harder than her husband's.

Consider for example the lot of peasant women. In France they make up the majority of women engaged in productive labour; and they are generally married. Customs vary in different regions: the Norman peasant woman presides at meals, whereas the Corsican woman does not sit at table with the men; but everywhere, playing a most important part in the domestic economy, she shares the man's responsibilities, interests, and property; she is respected and often is in effective control—her situation recalls that of woman in the old agricultural communities. She often has more moral prestige than her husband, but she lives in fact a much harder life. She has exclusive care of garden, sheepfold, pigpen, and so on, and shares in the hard labour of stablework, planting, ploughing, weeding and haying; she spades, reaps, picks grapes and sometimes helps load and unload wagons with hay, wood and so forth. She cooks, keeps house, does washing, mending and the like. She takes on the heavy duties of maternity and child care. She gets up at dawn, feeds the poultry and other small livestock, serves breakfast to the men, goes to work in field, wood, or garden; she draws water, serves a second meal, washes the dishes, works in the fields until time for dinner, and afterwards spends the evening mending, cleaning, knitting and what not. Having no time to care for her own health, even when pregnant, she soon gets misshapen; she is prematurely withered and worn out, gnawed by sickness. The compensations man finds in occasional social life are denied to her: he goes in to town on Sundays and market days, meets other men, drinks and plays cards in cafés, goes hunting and fishing. She stays at home on the farm and knows no leisure. Only the well-to-do peasant women, who have servants or can avoid field labour, lead a well-balanced life: they are socially honoured and at home exert a great deal of authority without being crushed by work. But for the most part rural labour reduces woman to the condition of a beast of burden.

The business-woman and the female employer who runs a small enterprise have always been among the privileged; they are the only women recognized since the Middle Ages by the Code as having civil rights and powers. Female grocers, dairy keepers, landladies, tobacconists have a position equivalent to man's; as spinsters or widows, they can in themselves constitute a legal firm; married, they have the same independence as their husbands. Fortunately their work can be carried on in the place where they live, and usually it is not too absorbing.

Things are quite otherwise for the woman worker or employee, the secretary, the saleswoman, all of whom go to work outside the home. It is much more difficult for them to combine their employment with household duties, which would seem to require at least three and a half hours a day, with perhaps six hours on Sunday—a good deal to add to the hours in factory or office. As for the learned professions, even if women lawyers, doctors, and professors obtain some housekeeping help, the home and children are for them also a burden that is a heavy handicap. In America domestic work is simplified by ingenious gadgets; but the elegant appearance required of the working-woman imposes upon her another obligation, and she remains responsible for house and children.

Furthermore, the woman who seeks independence through work has less favourable possibilities than her masculine competitors. Her wages in most jobs are lower than those of men; her tasks are less specialized and therefore not so well paid as those of skilled labourers; and for equal work she does not get equal pay. Because of the fact that she is a newcomer in the universe of males, she has fewer chances for success than they have. Men and women alike hate to be under the orders of a woman; they always show more confidence in a man; to be a woman is, if not a defect, at least a peculiarity. In order to 'arrive', it is well for a woman to make sure of masculine backing. Men unquestionably occupy the most advantageous places, hold the most important posts. It is essential to emphasize the fact that men and women, economically speaking, constitute two castes.[1]

The fact that governs woman's actual condition is the obstinate survival of extremely antique traditions into the new civilization that is just appearing in vague outline. That is what is misunderstood by hasty observers who regard woman as not up to the possibilities now offered to her or again who see in these possibilities only dangerous temptations. The truth is that her situation is out of equilibrium, and for that reason it is very difficult for her to adapt herself to it. We open the factories, the offices, the faculties to woman, but we continue to hold that marriage is for her a most honourable career, freeing her from the need of any other participation in the collective life. As in primitive civilizations, the act of love is on her part a service for which she has the right to be more or less directly paid. Except in the Soviet Union,[2] modern woman is everywhere permitted to regard her body as capital for exploitation. Prostitution is tolerated,[3] gallantry encouraged. And the married woman is empowered to see to it that her husband supports her ; in addition she is clothed in a social dignity far superior to that of the spinster. The mores are far from conceding to the latter sexual possibili-

[1] In America the great fortunes often fall finally into women's hands : younger than their husbands, they survive them and inherit from them; but by that time they are getting old and rarely have the initiative to make new investments; they are enjoyers of income rather than proprietors. It is really men who handle the capital funds. At any rate, these privileged rich women make up only a tiny minority. In America, much more than in Europe, it is almost impossible for a woman to reach a high position as lawyer, doctor, etc.

[2] At least according to official doctrine.

[3] In Anglo-Saxon countries prostitution has never been regulated. Up to 1900 English and American common law did not regard it as an offence except when it made public scandal and created disorder. Since that date repression has been more or less rigorously imposed, more or less successfully, in England and in the various states of the United States, where legislation in the matter is very diverse. In France, after a long campaign for abolition, the law of April 13th, 1946, ordered the closing of licensed brothels and the intensifying of the struggle against procuring : 'Holding that the existence of these houses is incompatible with the essential principles of human dignity and the role awarded to woman in modern society.' But prostitution continues none the less to carry on. It is evident that the situation cannot be modified by negative and hypocritical measures.

ties equivalent to those of the bachelor male; in particular maternity is practically forbidden her, the unmarried mother remaining an object of scandal. How, indeed, could the myth of Cinderella[1] not keep all its validity? Everything still encourages the young girl to expect fortune and happiness from some Prince Charming rather than to attempt by herself their difficult and uncertain conquest. In particular she can hope to rise, thanks to him, into a caste superior to her own, a miracle that could not be bought by the labour of her lifetime. But such a hope is a thing of evil because it divides her strength and her interests;[2] this division is perhaps woman's greatest handicap. Parents still bring up their daughter with a view to marriage rather than to furthering her personal development; she sees so many advantages in it that she herself wishes for it; the result is that she is often less specially trained, less solidly grounded than her brothers, she is less deeply involved in her profession. In this way she dooms herself to remain in its lower levels, to be inferior; and the vicious circle is formed: this professional inferiority reinforces her desire to find a husband.

Every benefit always has as its bad side some burden; but if the burden is too heavy, the benefit seems no longer to be anything more than a servitude. For the majority of labourers, labour today is a thankless drudgery, but in the case of woman this is not compensated for by a definite conquest of her social dignity, her freedom of behaviour, or her economic independence; it is natural for many women workers and employees to see in the right to work only an obligation from which marriage will deliver them. Because of the fact that she has taken on awareness of self, however, and because she can also free herself from marriage through a job, woman no longer accepts domestic subjection with docility. What she would hope is that the reconciliation of family life with a job should not require of her an exhausting, difficult performance. Even then, as long as the temptations of convenience exist—in the economic inequality that favours certain individuals and the recognized right of woman to sell herself to one of these privileged men—she will need to make a greater moral effort than would a man in choosing the road of independence. It has not been sufficiently realized that the temptation is also an obstacle, and even one of the most dan-

[1] Cf. PHILIP WYLIE, *Generation of Vipers* (Farrar, Straus & Co., 1942).

[2] We will return to this point at some length in Book Two.

161

F

gerous. Here a hoax is involved, since in fact there will be only one winner out of thousands in the lottery of marriage. The present epoch invites, even compels women to work; but is flashes before their eyes paradises of idleness and delight: it exalts the winners far above those who remain tied down to earth.

The privileged place held by men in economic life, their social usefulness, the prestige of marriage, the value of masculine backing, all this makes women wish ardently to please men. Women are still, for the most part, in a state of subjection. It follows that woman sees herself and makes her choices not in accordance with her true nature in itself, but as man defines her. So we must first go on to describe woman such as men have fancied her in their dreams, for what-in-men's-eyes-she-seems-to-be is one of the necessary factors in her real situation.

PART III

MYTHS

CHAPTER I

DREAMS, FEARS, IDOLS

HISTORY has shown us that men have always kept in their hands all concrete powers ; since the earliest days of the patriarchate they have thought best to keep woman in a state of dependence ; their codes of law have been set up against her ; and thus she has been definitely established as the Other. This arrangement suited the economic interests of the males ; but it conformed also to their ontological and moral pretensions. Once the subject seeks to assert himself, the Other, who limits and denies him, is none the less a necessity to him : he attains himself only through that reality which he is not, which is something other than himself. That is why man's life is never abundance and quietude ; it is dearth and activity, it is struggle. Before him, man encounters Nature ; he has some hold upon her, he endeavours to mould her to his desire. But she cannot fill his needs. Either she appears simply as a purely impersonal opposition, she is an obstacle and remains a stranger ; or she submits passively to man's will and permits assimilation, so that he takes possession of her only through consuming her—that is, through destroying her. In both cases he remains alone ; he is alone when he touches a stone, alone when he devours a fruit. There can be no presence of an other unless the other is also present in and for himself : which is to say that true alterity—otherness—is that of a consciousness separate from mine and substantially identical with mine.

It is the existence of other men that tears each man out of his immanence and enables him to fulfil the truth of his being, to complete himself through transcendence, through escape towards some objective, through enterprise. But this liberty not my own, while assuring mine, also conflicts with it : there is the tragedy of the unfortunate human consciousness ; each separate conscious being aspires to set himself up alone as sovereign subject. Each tries to fulfil himself by reducing the other to slavery. But the slave, though he works and fears, senses himself somehow as the essential ; and, by a dialectical inversion, it is the master who seems to be inessential. It is possible to rise above this conflict if each individual freely recognizes the other, each regarding himself and the other simultaneously as object and as subject in a reciprocal manner. But friendship and generosity, which alone permit in actuality this recognition of free beings, are not facile virtues ; they are assuredly man's highest achievement, and through that achievement he is to be found in his true nature. But this true nature is that of a struggle unceasingly begun, unceasingly abolished ; it requires man to outdo himself at every moment. We might put it in other words and say that man attains an authentically moral attitude when he renounces *mere being* to assume his position as an existent ; through this transformation also he renounces all possession, for possession is one way of seeking mere being ; but the transformation through which he attains true wisdom is never done, it is necessary to make it without ceasing, it demands a constant tension. And so, quite unable to fulfil himself in solitude, man is incessantly in danger in his relations with his fellows : his life is a difficult enterprise with success never assured.

But he does not like difficulty ; he is afraid of danger. He aspires in contradictory fashion both to life and to repose, to existence and to merely being ; he knows full well that 'trouble of spirit' is the price of development, that his distance from the object is the price of his nearness to himself ; but he dreams of quiet in disquiet and of an opaque plenitude that nevertheless would be endowed with consciousness. This dream incarnated is precisely woman ; she is the wished-for intermediary between nature, the stranger to man, and the fellow who is too closely identical.[1] She opposes him with neither the hostile silence of nature nor the hard requirement of a reciprocal relation ; through a unique privilege she is a conscious being and yet it seems possible to possess her in the

[1] '...Woman is not the useless replica of man, but rather the enchanted place where the living alliance between man and nature is brought about. If she should disappear, men would be alone, strangers lacking passports in an icy world. She is the earth itself raised to life's summit, the earth become sensitive and joyous; and without her, for man the earth is mute and dead,' writes MICHEL CARROUGES ('Les Pouvoirs de la femme', *Cahiers du Sud*, No. 292).

flesh. Thanks to her, there is a means for escaping that implacable dialectic of master and slave which has its source in the reciprocity that exists between free beings.

We have seen that there were not at first free women whom the males had enslaved nor were there even castes based on sex. To regard woman simply as a slave is a mistake; there were women among the slaves, to be sure, but there have always been free women—that is, women of religious and social dignity. They accepted man's sovereignty and he did not feel menaced by a revolt that could make of him in turn the object. Women thus seems to be the inessential who never goes back to being the essential, to be the absolute Other, without reciprocity. This conviction is dear to the male, and every creation myth has expressed it, among others the legend of Genesis, which, through Christianity, has been kept alive in Western civilization. Eve was not fashioned at the same time as the man; she was not fabricated from a different substance, nor of the same clay as was used to model Adam: she was taken from the flank of the first male. Not even her birth was independent; God did not spontaneously choose to create her as an end in herself and in order to be worshipped directly by her in return for it. She was destined by Him for man; it was to rescue Adam from loneliness that He gave her to him, in her mate was her origin and her purpose; she was his complement in the order of the inessential. Thus she appeared in the guise of privileged prey. She was nature elevated to transparency of consciousness; she was a conscious being, but naturally submissive. And therein lies the wondrous hope that man has often put in women: he hopes to fulfil himself as a being by carnally possessing a being, but at the same time confirming his sense of freedom through the docility of a free person. No one would consent to be a woman, but every man wants women to exist. 'Thank God for having created woman.' 'Nature is good since she has given women to men.' In such expressions man once more asserts with naive arrogance that his presence in this world is an ineluctable fact and a right, that of woman a mere accident—but a very happy accident. Appearing as the Other, woman appears at the same time as an abundance of being in contrast to that existence the nothingness of which man senses in himself; the Other, being regarded as the object in the eyes of the subject, is regarded as *en soi*; therefore as a being. In woman is incarnated in positive form the lack that the existent carries in his heart, and it is in seeking to be made whole through her that man hopes to attain self-realization.

She has not represented for him, however, the only incarnation of the Other, and she has not always kept the same important throughout the course of history. There have been moments when she has been eclipsed by other idols. When the City or the State devours the citizen, it is no longer possible for him to be occupied with his personal destiny. Being dedicated to the State, the Spartan woman's condition was above that of other Greek women. But it is also true that she was transfigured by no masculine dream. The cult of the leader, whether he be Napoleon, Mussolini, or Hitler, excludes all other cults. In military dictatorships, in totalitarian regimes, woman is no longer a privileged object. It is understandable that woman should be deified in a rich country where the citizens are none too certain of the meaning of life: thus it is in America. On the other hand, socialist ideologies, which assert the equality of all human beings, refuse now and for the future to permit any human category to be object or idol: in the authentically democratic society proclaimed by Marx there is no place for the Other. Few men, however, conform exactly to the militant, disciplined figure they have chosen to be; to the degree in which they remain individuals, woman keeps in their eyes a special value. I have seen letters written by German soldiers to French prostitutes in which, in spite of Nazism, the ingrained tradition of virgin purity was naively confirmed. Communist writers, like Aragon in France and Vittorini in Italy, give a place of the first rank in their works to woman, whether mistress or mother. Perhaps the myth of woman will some day be extinguished; the more women assert themselves as human beings, the more the marvellous quality of the Other will die out in them. But today it still exists in the heart of every man.

A myth always implies a subject who projects his hopes and his fears towards a sky of transcendence. Women do not set themselves up as Subject and hence have erected no virile myth in which their projects are reflected; they have no religion or poetry of their own: they still dream through the dreams of men. Gods made by males are the gods they worship. Men have shaped for their own exaltation great virile figures: Hercules, Prometheus, Parsifal; woman has only a secondary part to play in the destiny of these heroes. No doubt there are conventional figures of man caught in his relations to woman: the father, the seducer, the husband, the jealous lover, the good son, the wayward son; but they have all been established by men, and they lack the dignity of myth, being hardly more than clichés. Whereas woman is defined exclusively in her relation to man. The asymmetry of the categories—male and female—is made manifest in the unilateral form of sexual myths. We sometimes say 'the sex' to designate woman; she is the flesh, its delights and dangers. The truth that for woman man is sex and carnality has never been proclaimed because there is no one to proclaim it. Representation of the world, like the world itself, is the work of men; they describe it from their own point of view, which they confuse with absolute truth.

It is always difficult to describe a myth; it cannot be grasped or encompassed; it haunts the human consciousness without ever appearing before it in fixed form. The myth is so various, so contradictory, that at first its unity is not discerned: Delilah and Judith, Aspasia and Lucretia, Pandora and Athena—woman is at once Eve and the Virgin Mary. She is an idol, a servant, the source of life, a power of darkness; she is the elemental silence of truth, she is artifice, gossip, and falsehood; she is healing presence and sorceress; she is man's prey, his downfall, she is everything that he is not and that he longs for, his negation and his *raison d'être*.

'To be a woman,' says Kierkegaard in *Stages on the Road of Life,* 'is something so strange, so confused, so complicated, that no one predicate comes near expressing it and that the multiple predicates that one would like to use are so contradictory that only a woman could put up with it.' This comes from not regarding woman positively, such as she seems to herself to be, but negatively, such as she appears to man. For if woman is not the only *Other*, it remains none the less true that she is always defined as the Other. And her ambiguity is just that of the concept of the Other: it is that of the human situation in so far as it is defined in its relation with the Other. As I have already said, the Other is Evil; but being necessary to the Good, it turns into the Good; through it I attain to the Whole, but it also separates me therefrom; it is the gateway to the infinite and the measure of my finite nature. And here lies the reason why woman incarnates no stable concept; through her is made unceasingly the passage from hope to frustration, from hate to love, from good to evil, from evil to good. Under whatever aspect we may consider her, it is this ambivalence that strikes us first.

169

Man seeks in woman the Other as Nature and as his fellow being. But we know what ambivalent feelings Nature inspires in man. He exploits her, but she crushes him, he is born of her and dies in her; she is the source of his being and the realm that he subjugates to his will; Nature is a vein of gross material in which the soul is imprisoned, and she is the supreme reality; she is contingence and Idea, the finite and the whole; she is what opposes the Spirit, and the Spirit itself. Now ally, now enemy, she appears as the dark chaos from whence life itself wells up, as this life itself, and as the over-yonder towards which life tends. Woman sums up nature as Mother, Wife, and Idea; these forms now mingle and now conflict, and each of them wears a double visage.

Man has his roots deep in Nature; he has been engendered like the animals and plants; he well knows that he exists only so far as he lives. But since the coming of the patriarchate, Life has worn in his eyes a double aspect: it is consciousness, will, transcendence, it is the spirit; and it is matter, passivity, immanence, it is the flesh. Aeschylus, Aristotle, Hippocrates proclaimed that on earth as on Olympus it is the male principle that is truly creative: from it came form, number, movement; grain grows and multiplies through Demeter's care, but the origin of the grain and its verity lie in Zeus; woman's fecundity is regarded as only a passive quality. She is the earth, and man the seed; she is Water and he is Fire. Creation has often been imagined as the marriage of fire and water; it is warmth and moisture that give rise to living things; the Sun is the husband of the Sea; the Sun, fire, are male divinities; and the Sea is one of the most nearly universal of maternal symbols. Passively the waters accept the fertilizing action of the flaming radiations. So also the sod, broken by the ploughman's labour, passively receives the seeds within its furrows. But it plays a necessary part: it supports the living germ, protects it and furnishes the substance for its growth. And that is why man continued to worship the goddesses of fecundity, even after the Great Mother was dethroned;[1] he is indebted to Cybele for his crops, his herds, his whole prosperity. He even owes his own life to her. He sings the praises of water no less than fire. 'Glory to the sea! Glory to its waves surrounded with sacred fire! Glory to the wave! Glory

[1] 'I sing the earth, firmly founded mother of all, venerable grandmother, supporting on her soil all that lives,' says a Homeric hymn. And Aeschylus also glorifies the land which 'brings forth all beings, supports them, and then receives in turn their fertile seed'.

170

to the fire! Glory to the strange adventure,' cries Goethe in the Second Part of *Faust*. Man venerates the Earth: 'The matron Clay', as Blake calls her. A prophet of India advises his disciples not to spade the earth, for 'it is a sin to wound or to cut, to tear the mother of us all in the labours of cultivation ... Shall I go take a knife and plunge it into my mother's breast? ... Shall I hack at her flesh to reach her bones? ...How dare I cut off my mother's hair?' In central India the Baidya also consider it a sin to 'tear their earth mother's breast with the plough'. Inversely, Aeschylus says of Oedipus that he 'dared to seed the sacred furrow wherein he was formed'. Sophocles speaks of 'paternal furrows' and of the 'ploughman, master of a distant field that he visits only once, at the time of sowing'. The loved one of an Egyptian song declares: 'I am the earth!' In Islamic texts woman is called 'field ... vineyard'. St. Francis of Assisi speaks in one of his hymns of 'our sister, the earth, our mother, keeping and caring for us, producing all kinds of fruits, with many-coloured flowers and with grass'. Michelet, taking the mud baths at Acqui, exclaimed: 'Dear mother of all! We are one. I came from you, to you I return! ...' And so it is in periods when there flourishes a vitalist romanticism that desires the triumph of Life over Spirit ; then the magical fertility of the land, of woman, seems to be more wonderful than the contrived operations of the male: then man dreams of losing himself anew in the maternal shadows that he may find there again the true sources of his being. The mother is the root which, sunk in the depths of the cosmos, can draw up its juices ; she is the fountain whence springs forth the living water, water that is also a nourishing milk, a warm spring, a mud made of earth and water, rich in restorative virtues.[1]

But more often man is in revolt against his carnal state ; he sees himself as a fallen god: his curse is to be fallen from a bright and ordered heaven into the chaotic shadows of his mother's womb. This fire, this pure and active exhalation in which he likes to recognize himself, is imprisoned by woman in the mud of the earth. He would be inevitable, like a pure Idea, like the One, the All, the absolute Spirit ; and he finds himself shut up in a body of limited powers, in a place and time he never chose, where he was not called for, useless, cumbersome, absurd. The contingency of all flesh is his own

---

[1] 'Literally, woman is Isis, fecund nature. She is the river and the river-bed, the root and the rose, the earth and the cherry tree, the vine-stock and the grape.' (CARROUGES, loc. cit.)

to suffer in his abandonment, in his unjustifiable needlessness. She also dooms him to death. This quivering jelly which is elaborated in the womb (the womb, secret and sealed like the tomb) evokes too clearly the soft viscosity of carrion for him not to turn shuddering away. Wherever life is in the making—germination, fermentation—it arouses disgust because it is made only in being destroyed; the slimy embryo begins the cycle that is completed in the putrefaction of death. Because he is horrified by needlessness and death, man feels horror at having been engendered; he would fain deny his animal ties; through the fact of his birth murderous Nature has a hold upon him.

Among primitive peoples childbirth is surrounded by the most severe taboos; in particular, the placenta must be carefully burned or thrown into the sea, for whoever should get possession of it would hold the fate of the newborn in his hands. That membranous mass by which the fetus grows is the sign of its dependency; when it is destroyed, the individual is enabled to tear himself from the living magma and become an autonomous being. The uncleanness of birth is reflected upon the mother. Leviticus and all the ancient codes impose rites of purification upon one who has given birth; and in many rural districts the ceremony of churching (blessing after childbirth) continues this tradition. We know the spontaneous embarrassment, often disguised under mocking laughter, felt by children, young girls, and men at sight of the pregnant abdomen: the swollen bosom of the woman with child. In museums the curious gaze at waxen embryos and preserved fetuses with the same morbid interest they show in a ravaged tomb. With all the respect thrown around it by society, the function of gestation still inspires a spontaneous feeling of revulsion. And if the little boy remains in early childhood sensually attached to the maternal flesh, when he grows older, becomes socialized, and takes note of his individual existence, this same flesh frightens him; he would ignore it and see in his mother only a moral personage. If he is anxious to believe her pure and chaste, it is less because of amorous jealousy than because of his refusal to see her as a body. The adolescent is embarrassed, he blushes, if while with his companions he happens to meet his mother, his sisters, any of his female relatives: it is because their presence calls him back to those realms of immanence whence he would fly, exposes roots from which he would tear himself loose. The little boy's irritation when his mother kisses and cajoles him has the same

172

significance ; he disowns family, mother, maternal bosom. He would like to have sprung into the world, like Athena fully grown, fully armed, invulnerable.[1] To have been conceived and then born an infant is the curse that hangs over his destiny, the impurity that contaminates his being. And, too, it is the announcement of his death. The cult of germination has always been associated with the cult of the dead. The Earth Mother engulfs the bones of her children. They are women— the Parcae, the Moirai—who weave the destiny of mankind ; but it is they, also, who cut the threads. In most popular representations Death is a woman, and it is for women to bewail the dead because death is their work.[2]

Thus the Woman-Mother has a face of shadows: she is the chaos whence all have come and whither all must one day return ; she is Nothingness. In the Night are confused together the multiple aspects of the world which daylight reveals: night of spirit confined in the generality and opacity of matter, night of sleep and of nothingness. In the deeps of the sea it is night: woman is the *Mare tenebrarum,* dreaded by navigators of old ; it is night in the entrails of the earth. Man is frightened of this night, the reverse of fecundity, which threatens to swallow him up. He aspires to the sky, to the light, to the sunny summits, to the pure and crystalline frigidity of the blue sky ; and under his feet there is a moist, warm, and darkling gulf ready to draw him down ; in many a legend do we see the hero lost for ever as he falls back into the maternal shadows —cave, abyss, hell.

But here again is the play of ambivalence: if germination is always associated with death, so is death with fecundity. Hated death appears as a new birth, and then it becomes blessed. The dead hero is resurrected, like Osiris, each spring, and he is regenerated by a new birth. Man's highest hope, says Jung, in *Metamorphoses of the Libido,* 'is that the dark waters of death become the waters of life, that death and its cold embrace be the motherly bosom, which like the ocean, although engulfing the sun, gives birth to it again within its depths'. A theme common to numerous mythologies is the burial of the sun-god in the bosom of the ocean and his

[1] See below (p. 223) the study of Montherlant, who embodies this attitude in exemplary fashion.

[2] Demeter typifies the *mater dolorosa.* But other goddesses— Ishtar, Artemis—are cruel. Kali holds in her hand a cranium filled with blood. A Hindu poet addresses her: 'The heads of thy newly killed sons hang like a necklace about thy neck ... Thy form is beautiful like rain clouds, thy feet are soiled with blood.'

dazzling reappearance. And man at once wants to live but longs for repose and sleep and nothingness. He does not wish he were immortal, and so he can learn to love death. Nietzsche writes: 'Inorganic matter is the maternal bosom. To be freed of life is to become true again, it is to achieve perfection. Whoever should understand that would consider it a joy to return to the unfeeling dust.' Chaucer put his prayer into the mouth of an old man unable to die:

> With my staff, night and day
> I strike on the ground, my mother's doorway,
> And I say: Ah, mother dear, let me in.

Man would fain affirm his individual existence and rest with pride on his 'essential difference', but he wishes also to break through the barriers of the ego, to mingle with the water, the night, with Nothingness, with the Whole. Woman condemns man to finitude, but she also enables him to exceed his own limits; and hence comes the equivocal magic with which she is endued.

In all civilizations and still in our day woman inspires man with horror; it is the horror of his own carnal contingence, which he projects upon her. The little girl, not yet in puberty, carries no menace, she is under no taboo and has no sacred character. In many primitive societies her very sex seems innocent: erotic games are allowed from infancy between boys and girls. But on the day she can reproduce, woman becomes impure; and rigorous taboos surround the menstruating female. Leviticus gives elaborate regulations, and many primitive societies have similar rules regarding isolation and purification. In matriarchal societies the powers attributed to menstruation were ambivalent: the flow could upset social activities and ruin crops; but it was also used in love potions and medicines. Even today certain Indians put in the bow of the boat a mass of fibre soaked in menstrual blood, to combat river demons. But since patriarchal times only evil powers have been attributed to the feminine flow. Pliny said that a menstruating woman ruins crops, destroys gardens, kills bees, and so on; and that if she touches wine, it becomes vinegar; milk is soured, and the like. An ancient English poet put the same notion into rhyme:

> Oh! Menstruating woman, thou'st a fiend
> From whom all nature should be screened!

Such beliefs have survived with considerable power into recent times. In 1878 it was declared in the *British Medical Journal* that 'it is an undoubted fact that meat spoils when touched by menstruating women', and cases were cited from personal observation. And at the beginning of this century a rule forbade women having 'the curse' to enter the refineries of northern France, for that would cause the sugar to blacken. These ideas still persist in rural districts, where every cook knows that a mayonnaise will not be successful if a menstruating woman is about; some rustics believe cider will not ferment, others that bacon cannot be salted and will spoil under these circumstances. A few vaguely factual reports may offer some slight support for such beliefs; but it is obvious from their importance and universality that they must have had a superstitious or mystical origin. Certainly there is more here than reaction to blood in general, sacred as it is. But menstrual blood is peculiar, it represents the essence of femininity. Hence it can supposedly bring harm to the woman herself if misused by others. According to C. Lévi-Strauss, among the Chago the girls are warned not to let anyone see any signs of the flow; clothes must be buried, and so on, to avoid danger. Leviticus likens menstruation to gonorrhea, and Vigny associates the notion of uncleanness with that of illness when he writes: 'Woman, sick child and twelve times impure.'

The periodic haemorrhage of woman is strangely timed with the lunar cycle; and the moon also is thought to have her dangerous caprices.[1] Woman is a part of that fearsome machinery which turns the planets and the sun in their courses, she is the prey of cosmic energies that rule the destiny of the stars and the tides, and of which men must undergo the disturbing radiations. But menstrual blood is supposed to act especially on organic substances, half way between matter and life: souring cream, spoiling meat, causing fermentation, decomposition; and this less because it is blood than because it issues from the genital organs. Without comprehending its exact function, people have realized that it is bound to the

[1] The moon is a source of fertility; it appears as 'master of women'; it is often believed that in the form of man or serpent it couples with women. The serpent is an epiphany of the moon; it sheds its skin and renews itself, it is immortal, it is an influence promoting fecundity and knowledge. It is the serpent that guards the sacred springs, the tree of life, the fountain of youth. But it is also the serpent that took from man his immortality. Persian and rabbinical traditions maintain that menstruation is to be attributed to the relations of the woman with the serpent.

reproduction of life: ignorant of the ovary, the ancients even saw in the menses the complement of the sperm. The blood, indeed, does not make woman impure; it is rather a sign of her impurity. It concerns generation, it flows from the parts where the fetus develops. Through menstrual blood is expressed the horror inspired in man by woman's fecundity.

One of the most rigorous taboos forbids all sexual relations with a woman in a state of menstrual impurity. In various cultures offenders have themselves been considered impure for certain periods, or they have been required to undergo severe penance; it has been supposed that masculine energy and vitality would be destroyed because the feminine principle is then at its maximum of force. More vaguely, man finds it repugnant to come upon the dreaded essence of the mother in the woman he possesses; he is determined to dissociate these two aspects of femininity. Hence the universal law prohibiting incest,[1] expressed in the rule of exogamy or in more modern forms; this is why man tends to keep away from woman at the times when she is especially taken up with her reproductive role: during her menses, when she is pregnant, in lactation. The Oedipus complex—which should be redescribed—does not deny this attitude, but on the contrary implies it. Man is on the defensive against woman in so far as she represents the vague source of the world and obscure organic development.

It is in this guise also, however, that woman enables her group, separated from the cosmos and the gods, to remain in communication with them. Today she still assures the fertility of the fields among the Bedouins and the Iroquois; in ancient Greece she heard the subterranean voices; she caught the language of winds and trees: she was Pythia, sibyl, prophetess; the dead and the gods spoke through her mouth. She keeps today these powers of divination: she is medium, reader of palms and cards, chairvoyant, inspired; she hears voices, sees apparitions. When men feel the need to plunge again into the midst of plant and animal life—as Antaeus touched the earth to renew his strength—they make appeal to woman. All

---

[1] According to the view of a sociologist, G. P. MURDOCK, in *Social Structure* (Macmillan, 1949), incest prohibition can be fully accounted for only by a complex theory, involving factors contributed by psychoanalysis, sociology, cultural anthropology, and behaviouristic psychology. No simple explanation, like 'instinct', or 'familiar association', or 'fear of inbreeding', is at all satisfactory.—TR.